# WE ARE SISTERS

August 31, 2007

Dearest Phyllis,

I loved this book so much I used it as a Relief Society Book Review. I laughed. I cried. It reminds me of a visit with you.

We are sisters...
Happy Birthday!
Eternal love,
Ila and Clare

OTHER BOOKS AND AUDIO BOOKS
BY MARILYNNE TODD LINFORD:

*Sisters in Zion*

# WE ARE SISTERS

*Inspiration for Women*

Marilynne Todd Linford

Covenant

Cover image *Intangible* © Anita Robbins.

Cover design copyrighted 2007 by Covenant Communications, Inc.

Published by Covenant Communications, Inc.
American Fork, Utah



Printed in Canada
First Printing: March 2007

14 13 12 11 10 09 08 07 10 9 8 7 6 5 4 3 2 1

ISBN 978-1-59811-345-7

# PREFACE AND ACKNOWLEDGMENTS

Every month for the past seven years, I've written a one-page message for the sisters in my ward. It's been an unofficial calling from my Relief Society presidents—Sue Smith, Carol Pia, and Carole Kirk. I've enjoyed writing these messages and have written with the prayer that the words would be beneficial to some sister in the ward. When Covenant Communications saw a broader purpose and wider audience for the messages, I prayed to know your needs. Several times as new topics came to mind, thoughts flowed so simply and completely it's as though I've been an observer watching the words appear on the computer screen without forethought or plan. All the so-so work is mine; everything filled with the Spirit came through the Spirit. At these sacred times, I've bowed my head and given thanks to be the first to read the beautiful words.

After *Sisters in Zion* had been on the market for several months, I started hearing the same comment from readers. "I love your book," they'd say, "especially the short chapters!" You'll like that about this book, too, because the average length of each chapter is about a thousand words. I hope you'll also like the variety. All are for women. Some are specifically for young women, some are for mothers, some are ideas for family home evenings, some are for fun, and some are essays I hope men will read. All in all, I hope some will resonate and give you a spiritual boost.

I want to express love and gratitude to my Heavenly Father, my Savior, and to the Holy Ghost for the priesthood, temples, scriptures, commandments, Apostles and prophets, tender mercies, and promptings, to name just a few of the blessings of the gospel of Jesus Christ.

I thank my mother for her incredible stability and love. I'm thankful to my parents for giving me seven siblings. As the oldest of that tribe and the mother of eight, I've had the opportunity to quasi or actually parent fifteen children. And, as expected, just when I thought I finally got something right, a new mothering challenge appeared. I'm grateful for my husband, who willingly edits everything I write. How I appreciate his love and testimony. I'm grateful for our children and grandchildren, for their love and support and for the good times we have together. I'm thankful for my sisters, who are dearest friends, and for my friends, who are like dear sisters.

I extend specific thanks and appreciation to my editor, friend, and daughter, Elizabeth Lehnhof, who skillfully and unrelentingly identified the so-so portions of the book and made them less so-so. We've worked with the hope that as you read this book you'll laugh and cry and reflect on the adventure of being a sister in Zion at this complex and exciting time in the history of the world.

# TUNING IN TO TENDER MERCIES

Can you measure Heavenly Father's love for you by your health, wealth, or status? Would you know He loves you if you had a "Brady Bunch" childhood with loving parents, siblings, and a maid? Or if you married the man of your dreams and had the number of children you wanted, when you wanted them? Or if there was never an angry word in your marriage and your children were always healthy and obedient? Is your reward for loving the Lord a beautiful mortgage-free home and a bulging portfolio of stocks, bonds, and real estate?

We tend to measure God's love in tangibles—houses, cars, vacations, clothes, diplomas, promotions. We crave constant divine reinforcement and believe Heavenly Father when He says that He delights in blessing those who love Him. His ways, however, are not our ways. He has an expansive repertoire of alternative ways to bless His children—to teach, refine, and bring as many as are willing back into His glory. It's easy to identify His hand in the abundance—but when adversity comes, we yearn to know that He is also in the adversity. Is there a way during trials that you can know you yet register on His omniscient radar screen?

Elder David A. Bednar brought to our attention the scriptural phrase, "tender mercies" (see "The Tender Mercies of the Lord," *Ensign,* May, 2005, 99). *Tender mercies* are the blips on the radar screen that let us know Heavenly Father is aware of us. The phrase is found in both the Old Testament and the Book of Mormon verses (emphasis added).

- "Great are thy *tender mercies,* O LORD" (Psalms 119:156).
- "The LORD is good to all: and his *tender mercies* are over all his works" (Psalms 145:9).

- "I, Nephi, will show unto you that the *tender mercies* of the Lord are over all those whom he hath chosen, because of their faith . . ." (1 Nephi 1:20).
- "I began to pray unto the Lord that he would have mercy on me, according to the multitude of his *tender mercies*" (1 Nephi 8:8).

Elder Bednar defined tender mercies with an example. Just before he delivered his first-ever general conference address as an Apostle, the congregation stood and sang his favorite hymn, "Redeemer of Israel." "I knew . . . I was experiencing . . . a tender mercy. A loving Savior was sending me a most personal and timely message of comfort and reassurance. . . . Some may count this experience as simply a nice coincidence, but I testify that the tender mercies of the Lord are real and that they do not occur randomly or merely by coincidence" ("The Tender Mercies of the Lord," 99).

Tender mercies are perfectly suited and precision-timed spiritual messages. Tender mercies happen to faithful Saints experiencing the ups and downs and sideways of life. The problem with tender mercies *is not that they don't happen; it's that they go unnoticed or are explained away.*

Businessman Craig Brown tells the story of being in Philadelphia on a business trip and stepping onto an elevator to see President Thomas S. Monson. In that quick elevator ride, Craig had a moment to establish a commonality with President Monson and to receive a needed boost. Craig felt watched over and blessed by this "chance" meeting.

In saying goodbye to President Monson, Craig told him, "President Monson, meeting you here is like one of those coincidences you talk about in General Conference."

President Monson smiled and said, "Oh, Brother Brown, I don't believe in coincidences."

A Relief Society president heard Elder Bednar's talk and wondered, "Have I ever experienced a tender mercy?" After thinking about it, she knew she had; she just hadn't realized they had a name. As she identified a few, she realized she'd been unaware of many others. She decided to start asking Heavenly Father in prayer to help her better recognize His tender mercies. After hearing her tell her story, this little rhyme came to my mind:

In Father's tender mercies
A signature is etched;
His timing, peace, and charity
Reveal His arm outstretched.

Are Father's tender mercies
Coincidences? No!
They evidence, in sacred ways,
Your needs by Him are known.

As we tune in to tender mercies, it becomes obvious that each of us continually registers on His divine radar screen. May the tender mercies in your life be evidence of how mindful your Father in Heaven is of you—and may this assurance be part of your faith in Him and your love for Him.

# LOVE IN PRINCIPLE AND ACTION

I hope all of us have experienced love—that sublime emotion that helps us experience a little of what our Heavenly Father and our Savior exemplify so well. Sometimes love becomes so much a part of our lives that we don't stop to think about how love is actually demonstrated. There are many ways in which love is shown—and by identifying those ways, we can increase our own ability to show love.

**Love is shown in loving others' children.** In a unique book titled *Twelve Mormon Homes* by Elizabeth Wood Kane (wife of Thomas L. Kane, the "friend of the Mormons"), there is an incredible vignette of a woman's love. The book, originally published in 1874, evolved from notes Elizabeth Kane took as she stayed in twelve different Latter-day Saint homes. Elizabeth and Thomas Kane, not members of the Church, were invited by Brigham Young to travel with him on his annual trek of approximately three hundred miles from Salt Lake City to St. George. Elizabeth's account gives her impressions of Latter-day Saint families in their own environments in 1872. Her experience in one of the twelve homes reads:

"While I talked with the Steerforth women over the glowing fire, I was idly wondering to which of the wives the different children belonged. The wee nursling and Noe were easily assigned to the little mother, but I puzzled myself vainly over the others who gathered about the pair with precisely the same caressing familiarity that we are accustomed to associate with the true filial instinct one and undivided. When I mentioned my difficulty they smiled, and asked me to point out those whom I thought belonged to each. I did so, and they laughed outright, telling me that the seven children belonged to the little mother. She had also lost five. 'Aunt Mary' was childless in name, but I never saw a mother of whom children seemed to be fonder, or who took more pride in the promising future of her 'natural offspring'" (Elizabeth Wood Kane, *Twelve Mormon Homes: Visited in Succession on a Journey through Utah to Arizona,* Everett Kooley, ed. [Salt Lake City: Signature Books Publishing, 1974], 46).

**Love is shown in gratitude.** I was at a rest home with a friend who had suffered a stroke, and we sat in the dining room as the patients were having lunch. An elderly woman sat across from me, and her nurse sat next to her. This elderly patient finished her meal, pushed back her chair, stood up, and said to the nurse, "How much do I owe you, sir?" Her nurse answered with a smile, "Nothing, it's on the house." Not understanding, the woman looked at him with pleading eyes. "I really don't have any money, but my daughter will pay you when she comes. How much do I owe?" "Nothing," the nurse repeated, "you owe nothing." The woman looked at the nurse with inexpressible thanksgiving, grabbed his arm, and said, "God bless you, my boy. Tell me your name and I will pray for you every day."

**Love is shown in finding commonalities.** Leah was serving in the Relief Society presidency at an assisted-living home. She went each Sunday for sacrament meeting and each Wednesday for Relief Society. Her duties included bringing the sisters to the recreation room for meetings, and she had to begin thirty minutes before the meetings started. Some of the residents were in their wheelchairs and ready to go, but others needed help putting on shoes or getting out of bed. Still others declined the invitation to come to church. One woman—Rachel, who was more physically able than the others—always claimed that she couldn't come to the church meeting because her sister was coming to see her. Week after week it was the same: "My sister is coming to see me."

Leah decided to find out if Rachel's sister did, in fact, come. The staff at the rest home said that to their knowledge, Rachel had never had a visitor. While driving by the assisted-living center, Leah often noticed Rachel standing in front of the home watching the cars go by. Leah wondered if she was waiting and hoping her sister would come. Leah wondered if she even had a sister.

The following Wednesday, Leah went into Rachel's room and asked her to come to Relief Society. "No, I can't," she responded as usual, "my sister is coming to see me." Inspiration filling her heart, Leah took Rachel by the arm and said," Rachel, my name is Leah, and in the Bible it says that Leah and Rachel are sisters. I am your sister. Come with me to Relief Society." Rachel's eyes brightened, and she allowed herself to be led to the meeting room that day and on the subsequent Sundays and Wednesdays.

**Love is shown in overlooking prejudices.** In the early 1970s we lived in Epsom, Surrey, England. One day we decided to travel about four hours away to a village that had been home to the Linford ancestors. As we arrived we immediately saw the cemetery adjacent to the church. We pulled into a small parking space in front of the church, and Richard left me and the children in the car while he went to the cemetery to read the names on headstones.

Soon I felt someone watching us. I looked up and saw a woman standing in her second-story window, observing all that was going on. A few minutes later I looked up again; she was still watching us. I thought perhaps we were in a reserved parking space and that I should move the car, but when I looked up to the window again, she was gone. Soon she was standing next to the car. She looked in the car window and said, "You look hot and tired. Would you like a drink of squash?" (Squash is an English drink made with fruit-flavored concentrate.) I thanked her and tried to refuse, but she wouldn't hear of it. Soon she was back, carrying a pitcher of squash and empty yogurt cups for all of us to drink from. She offered her bathroom to the children and made every effort to welcome us to her town.

When Richard came back to the car, the woman told us she was the caretaker of the church and asked if we would like to see it. She showed us the little chapel and told us how the reverend's picture used to be above the pulpit. She explained that she had his picture removed and the words "In Memory of Our Lord" put in its place. Then we followed her into the children's Sunday school room. I sensed a tense moment coming, and soon the question came: "Are you Baptist, too?"

Richard answered, "No, we are Mormons."

"Mormons?" she gasped in horror.

The cordial atmosphere changed one hundred and eighty degrees. Her feelings were obvious. She had befriended Mormons! Mormons were in her church. She quickly ushered us out of the room and up the stairs. She couldn't get rid of us fast enough. She wanted us out—out of her sacred place. We hurriedly climbed in the car, backed up, and began to drive away. I looked back. "Stop, Richard," I said. "She's running after us." She got to the car, huffing and puffing, looked in at all of us one by one, and, collecting the finest within her, said, "But I love you anyway." She waved as we drove away.

# WATERING YOUR NEIGHBOR'S LAWN*

We have lived next door to the same family for thirty years. Up until about ten years ago, when we got an automatic sprinkling system, I struggled to water a fifteen-foot strip of grass that adjoins our neighbor's lawn. Our neighbors have had automatic sprinklers for as long as we've lived next to them, and their lawn has always looked luxuriously green. The best I could do with my portable sprinkler was to keep our side barely presentable.

Since our neighbor's lawn was always green, I made sure that none of our water went on their side. Why should I help them when their lawn already looked so good? However, it was hard to water such a narrow section of grass, especially when I was being so stingy with the water.

Midway through one summer, I decided to allow our sprinkler water to freely go over the property line. To my surprise, our lawn quickly improved. The yellow grass along the property line disappeared, and our side didn't look so patchy. Soon there was no way to tell where our lawn began and the neighbor's ended—it was all one beautiful expanse.

But the benefit of watering our neighbor's lawn didn't end there. When our lawn started looking better, our neighbor started mowing our section of grass every time he mowed his own lawn. As a result, the property line is no longer apparent, not only because both sides are equally green, but also because the grass on each side is the same height—because it is mowed the same day.

This principle of watering your neighbor's lawn works in other situations to improve and bless lives. While three college-aged sisters were shopping together one afternoon, they all filled out entry blanks for a contest in which the winner would receive a thousand-dollar wardrobe. Several weeks later, the youngest sister was notified that she had won the prize. Elated, she began to plan a stylish, color-coordinated wardrobe. But then she thought of all the times she had borrowed her sisters' clothes. She wondered how she would feel wearing beautiful new clothes while her sisters wore the same old ones. After some deliberation, she decided to split the prize three ways. Her sisters were deeply touched. However, they insisted that their younger sister keep the prize for herself because she might never have another chance to build the basics of a real wardrobe. By "watering each other's lawns," the family avoided envy and contention and grew in love and unity.

A friend of mine was called as ward Primary president. While she was praying about which women should serve with her in the presidency, she felt impressed to keep the secretary from the previous presidency. However, the secretary seemed unhappy about serving with the new presidency and soon began to decline assignments and miss meetings. In an attempt to mollify her, the president stopped asking the secretary to help as much; in response, the secretary grew even more resistant and said, "Well, it's obvious you don't need me."

As the president prayed for help, she felt prompted to go to the secretary's house and simply tell her that she loved her. The tension was obvious when the secretary answered her door, but then the president said, "I just came over to tell you that I love you, and I hope we can work well together." From that day on, a change began to occur in the secretary. Not only did she start accepting more assignments and participating fully in the presidency, but over the years she and the president became close friends. Even after they were released, their friendship continued to grow. The president's effort to water the secretary's lawn paid off in a rich Church service experience and friendship for both.

The scriptures tell us, "Give, and it shall be given unto you; good measure, pressed down, and shaken together, and running over, shall men give into your bosom. For with the same measure that ye mete withal it shall be measured to you again" (Luke 6:38). When we water our neighbor's lawn, both we and our neighbor are blessed.

*First published as "Watering Our Neighbor's Lawn," *Ensign,* February 1996, 54. Used with permission.

# THE DAY JOHN LINFORD WAS RESCUED

English converts John Linford, his wife, Maria, and three of their four sons were members of the Willie Handcart Company. In late fall of 1856 when Elder Franklin D. Richards and a group of missionaries were returning from England, they passed the starving and freezing company on the trail when they were still more than three hundred miles from the Salt Lake Valley. Knowing that with their limited numbers they could be of little help, they hurried on to report to Brigham Young that more than a thousand saints were stranded in unseasonably cold weather on the high plains of Wyoming. In his talk the next day from the Bowery, Brigham Young said, "Many of our brethren and sisters are on the Plains with handcarts . . . they must be brought here, we must send assistance to them" (*Journal of Discourses,* 4:113).

The rescue parties arrived the same day John Linford died.

Can death be a rescue?

The Old Testament tells how Jonah struggled between right and wrong, how he refused to obey the Lord, and how he tried to dodge a mission call by sailing to Tarshish. We read that Jonah was cast into the tempestuous sea and nearly drowned before the whale swallowed him. Would you consider being swallowed alive a rescue in process?

W. W. Phelps, a once-trusted friend of Joseph Smith and faithful Church member, misused Church funds and was excommunicated. With vengeance in his heart, he joined the apostates and enemies of the Church in slandering the Prophet. His false accusations directly resulted in the attack on Haun's Mill and the four months Joseph Smith spent confined in Liberty Jail. Can excommunication be a rescue? Can being betrayed by a friend be a rescue? Can being jailed be a rescue?

I spent nearly a year suffering through breast cancer. I know what it is like to be sicker than sick and balder than bald. I know the loneliness, fear, and depression that accompany a life-threatening illness. Can illness be a rescue?

Can you be rescued by having a baby vomit just as you are leaving for an appointment? Can a rescue be in progress when employment is terminated or a business fails? Do rescues happen in every imaginable circumstance? The answer, of course, is yes.

The concept of rescue seems sure, but after I've seen or heard of a rescue, I sometimes ask myself why Betsy was rescued when Beverly didn't seem to be rescued. I don't have an answer, but perhaps Betsy responded to the rescue attempts and Beverly didn't. Or perhaps Beverly's rescue is still in progress.

The story of John Newton, a rebellious young Englishman who became a sailor in the 1700s, is a rescue story. While serving on a navy ship, John caused trouble, so he was traded to a slave ship, where he eventually became a ship commander. During this time, conditions on slave ships were so terrible that disease killed a high percentage of the slaves. John vowed to change that. On one trip he reached his goal of not a single slave losing his life during the voyage.

Around this time John prayed that he might find a more humane form of work, and he subsequently became too ill to ever command another ship (a rescue?). Due to the perils of sea travel and his illness, his thoughts turned to God. He eventually became a minister in Olney, England. His gratitude for the many times he was rescued physically and spiritually is well expressed in his much-loved words (see James Haskins, *Amazing Grace: The Story Behind the Song*, [Brookfield, Connecticut: Millbrook Press, 1992], 21–41):

> Amazing grace (how sweet the sound)
> That saved a wretch like me!
> I once was lost, but now am found,
> Was blind, but now I see.

As is obvious from John Newton's experience, rescues sometimes occur in increments or in multiple stages. This was the case with many of the members of the Willie and Martin handcart companies.

The sites where these two companies were stranded and first rescued lie within the Riverton Wyoming Stake boundaries. In 1991, 135 years after their physical rescue, Stake President Scott Lorimer told members of his stake something like this:

"A few years ago the Spirit of the Willie people began to rest upon me and I stood at this podium and asked you . . . to pray about the Willie project. . . . I was really asking for help in acquiring the Willie Handcart site near South Pass City.

"Looking back at what has happened I realize that what I really asked for . . . was that you would pray and help me and my counselors understand why the Spirit of the Willie people would not let us be" (*Remember,* Riverton Wyoming Stake, 1997, 145).

Finally, through a miraculous series of events, President Lorimer realized that much of the temple work for members of these two companies was incomplete. When the idea of a spiritual rescue was put to the members of the stake, they enthusiastically responded. During the next two years, they researched and performed temple ordinances for more than four thousand members of the Willie and Martin handcart companies and their descendants!

Having your temple work done vicariously is certainly a rescue; doing the work may be a rescue as well.

In the extremities of your unplanned, unwanted, seemingly unnecessary trials, have you cried to the Lord in prayer for relief? In response to such a cry in Liberty Jail, Joseph Smith received the most sublime answer while living in the most deplorable conditions possible. Both Joseph's pleas and the Lord's answer are found in the Doctrine and Covenants:

"O GOD, where art thou? And where is the pavilion that covereth thy hiding place?

"How long shall thy hand be stayed, and thine eye, yea thy pure eye, behold from the eternal heavens the wrongs of thy people and of thy servants, and thine ear be penetrated with their cries?

"Yea, O Lord, how long shall they suffer these wrongs and unlawful oppressions, before thine heart shall be softened toward them, and thy bowels be moved with compassion toward them?" (D&C 121:1–3).

The Lord's answer: "My son, peace be unto thy soul; thine adversity and thine afflictions shall be but a small moment;

"And then, if thou endure it well, God shall exalt thee on high; thou shalt triumph over all thy foes.

"Thy friends do stand by thee, and they shall hail thee again with warm hearts and friendly hands.

"Thou art not yet as Job; thy friends do not contend against thee, neither charge thee with transgression, as they did Job. . . .

"And if thou shouldst be cast into the pit, or into the hands of murderers, and the sentence of death passed upon thee; if thou be cast into the deep; if the billowing surge conspire against thee; if fierce winds become thine enemy; if the heavens gather blackness, and all the elements combine to hedge up the way; and above all, if the very jaws of hell shall gape open the mouth wide after thee, know thou, my son, that all these things shall give thee experience, and shall be for thy good" (D&C 121:7–10, 122:7).

Because I know God loves you, I know you have already experienced rescues and that your ultimate rescue is ongoing. I urge you to ask your Heavenly Father to open your eyes to the rescues in your life. A friend told me about the rescue of her son. It took an astonishing set of circumstances—as if actors were poised on the stage of his life at precisely the most critical moments to say and do their parts—for his rescue to occur. She savors these memories and recognizes God's mercy and grace focused on her and her little family.

Thank your Savior for the rescues you've experienced. He rescues both in life and death, health and sickness, peace and war, privilege and hardship. John Linford, Jonah, W. W. Phelps, John Newton, the members of the Willie and Martin handcart companies, and the Prophet Joseph Smith were all rescued. We all have been and will be rescued by He who saves. That is why He is called the Savior. Let's acknowledge Him and His amazing grace.

# THE FACTS AND FALLACIES ABOUT REPENTANCE

Repentance—taking the proper steps to forsake and be forgiven of our sins—allows us to take part in the Savior's Atonement and results in peace and joy in this life and in the life to come. Sincere repentance helps us prepare to live with our Heavenly Father. Thanks to scriptures and modern-day revelation, we know a lot about repentance. Here are some of the facts about this essential gospel principle:

**Fact 1:** Repentance is a commandment—"And he commandeth all men that they must repent . . ." (2 Nephi 9:23).

**Fact 2:** Repentance is the gospel. The gospel is called "the gospel of repentance" (D&C 13:1).

**Fact 3:** Repentance is essential because "no unclean thing can dwell with God" (1 Nephi 10:21).

**Fact 4:** The Atonement of Jesus Christ makes repentance possible. "For behold, I, God, have suffered these things for all, that they might not suffer if they would repent" (D&C 19:16).

**Fact 5:** Repentance is the eraser that rubs out sin as though it never happened. "Repent ye therefore . . . that your sins may be blotted out . . ." (Acts 3:19).

**Fact 6:** Repentance is the process whereby God forgets our sins: "saith the LORD . . . I will remember their sin no more" (Jeremiah 31:34).

**Fact 7:** Repentance covers all degrees of sin except the sin against the Holy Ghost. "Come now, and let us reason together, saith the LORD: though your sins be as scarlet, they shall be as white as snow; though they be red like crimson, they shall be as wool" (Isaiah 1:18).

**Fact 8:** Repentance is something every mortal must do: "For all have sinned, and come short of the glory of God" (Romans 3:23).

**Fact 9:** Repentance on one's deathbed is not repentance, because the repentant soul must be tried and proven. "By this ye may know if a man repenteth of his sins—behold, he will confess them and forsake them" (D&C 58:43). Amulek said, ". . . if ye have procrastinated the day of your repentance even until death, behold, ye have become subjected to the spirit of the devil, and he doth seal you his; therefore, the Spirit of the Lord hath withdrawn from you, and hath no place in you, and the devil hath all power over you; and this is the final state of the wicked" (Alma 34: 35).

**Fact 10:** Repentance is complete when you have a mighty change in your heart, when you have "no more disposition to do evil, but to do good continually" (Mosiah 5:2).

Those are some of the facts about repentance—the things we can know with certainty because they are taught in the scriptures. Unfortunately, there are also some fallacies about repentance that we might be tempted to believe. Let's take a look at three of the biggest deceptions about repentance:

**Fallacy #1: Repentance is easy.** If you are repenting of a small sin that you aren't very attached to and if you have good self-discipline and a strong desire to be free of the sin, I suppose it might be relatively easy to repent in that situation. But the more serious the sin, the more effort, time, humility, and sacrifice are required to fully repent. Also—and this is a very big ALSO—all sin is offensive to Heavenly Father, so any sin reduces the influence of the Holy Ghost in the sinner's life by increments, making repentance harder. That's a major concern, because the Holy Ghost's voice is already so still and small.

Elder Bruce R. McConkie wrote, "Through rebellion men sometimes place themselves in a position in which the Lord's Spirit will no longer strive with them. . ." (Bruce R. McConkie, *Mormon Doctrine* [Salt Lake City: Bookcraft, Inc., 1966], 631). And Elder James E. Talmage wrote: "To suppose that the soul who has willfully rejected the opportunity of repentance in this life will find it easy to repent there [in the spirit world] is contrary to reason. To procrastinate the day of repentance is to deliberately place ourselves in the power of the adversary" (James E. Talmage, *Articles of Faith* [Salt Lake City: The

Church of Jesus Christ of Latter-day Saints, 1976], 115).

**Fallacy #2: Repentance can wait.** Have you ever heard anyone joke that there's always time to repent? Actually, repentance is a time-sensitive commandment. Repentance is a precious gift for all of the reasons stated above and more, but one critical facet is not well understood. Repentance is like a coupon with an expiration date. Someone who thinks, "Oh, there's always time to repent" doesn't know or understand the plan. Alma explains it this way: "A space [meaning a period of time or perhaps even a place (the earth)] [was] granted unto man in which he might repent; therefore this life became a probationary state; a time to prepare to meet God; a time to prepare for that endless state . . . after the resurrection of the dead" (Alma 12:24). At some point after this life, the opportunity to sin and repent will be over. The Lord explained to Hosea that when the time to repent has expired, "repentance shall be hid from mine eyes" (Hosea 13:14).

**Fallacy #3: Repentance is optional.** Another misconception about repentance is that it is optional. It isn't. Justice is always going to be served. There are only two ways to make restitution for sin: 1. You can do all you can to make things right and humbly ask for the mercy of the Atonement to cover what you cannot; or 2. You can suffer the full consequences of sin and pay the debt yourself. The Savior explained the doctrine: "Verily I say unto thee, Thou shalt by no means come out thence [out of the spirit prison], till thou hast paid the uttermost farthing" (Matthew 5:26).

W. W. Phelps's contributions and apostasy are discussed in several places in this book. You'll remember that Phelps betrayed the Prophet Joseph Smith and that his actions led directly to the massacre at Haun's Mill and the Prophet's four-month confinement in Liberty Jail. You might also remember that Phelps felt he had sinned too greatly to ever receive forgiveness.

But I have not yet told the best part of this story. After Phelps sent a letter to Joseph Smith begging whatever degree of forgiveness he could grant, Joseph Smith wrote a letter in return. These two letters are a classic example of repentance and forgiveness. An excerpt of Phelps's letter is found on p. 122. Joseph's letter reads in part:

Dear Brother Phelps:

I must say that it is with no ordinary feelings I endeavor to write a few lines to you in answer to yours . . . at the same time I am rejoiced at the privilege granted me. . . .

It is true, that we have suffered much in consequence of your behavior—the cup of gall, already full enough for mortals to drink, was indeed filled to overflowing when you turned against us. One with whom we had oft taken sweet counsel together, and enjoyed many refreshing seasons from the Lord. . . .

Believing your confession to be real, and your repentance genuine, I shall be happy once again to give you the right hand of fellowship, and rejoice over the returning prodigal.

Your letter was read to the Saints last Sunday and an expression of their feeling was taken, when it was unanimously resolved, that W. W. Phelps should be received into fellowship.

Yours as ever, Joseph Smith, Jun.

P.S. Come on, dear brother, since the war is past,
For friends at first, are friends again at last.

# THE LORD'S ARITHMETIC

One Sunday morning when our children's ages ranged between five and nineteen, I arrived at church looking frazzled. How do I know? As I sat down in ward correlation meeting, the high priest group leader looked at me and said, "I didn't know it was windy outside."

Another Sunday morning, when our children's ages ranged between twenty-three and thirty-seven, I arrived at Church looking frazzled. How do I know? When I got to Relief Society, the Relief Society president greeted me at the door and asked about a couple of problems she knew we were experiencing with our children and grandchildren. I responded that the one whose house flooded was coping, and that the grandchild who had been in the hospital was home. She shook her head and said, "You must not be very good at math." "Why do you say that?" I asked. "Well, if you were good at math, you would realize that eight children times anything equals the potential for lots of troubles." Then she hugged me and we laughed.

Before you read further, I hope this message does not cause you heartache if you yearn for a large family but you aren't married or you have infertility issues or health concerns. You will be blessed for your righteous desires. Sarah, the wife of Abraham, is an excellent example of the Lord's arithmetic. She had only one child, and her posterity numbers as the sands of the sea.

So, is having a big family too stressful for today's frenetic world? According to the U.S. Census Bureau, the number of women who only have one child is soaring. "The number is going up every year," the bureau's Amara Bachu said. The statistic for women ages forty to forty-four who had only one child is "used as a marker for family size because women are assumed to be nearing the end of their child-bearing years. . . . This figure rose from 9.6% in 1980 to 17.3% in 1998. That's an 85% increase" (Ms. Bachu has written many interesting articles on various aspects of this issue that are available at www.census.gov/population/www/documentation/twps0020/twps0020.html).

An article in the *Christian Science Monitor* detailed the problem Russia is having with its birthrate compared to other countries. According to the article, it requires 2.4 children per couple to maintain a population. Russia's birthrate was 1.17 in 2004. "The average rate from 2000–2005 in the U.S., by contrast, was 2.0, according to U.N. figures, while Mexico, for example, weighed in at 2.4 and Italy at 1.3" ("A Second Baby? Russia's Mothers Aren't Persuaded," *Christian Science Monitor,* May 19, 2006).

According to the National Right to Life organization, 45 million babies were aborted in the United States from 1973 to 2000. According to the U.S. Census Bureau, "Birth rates are highest for women with the least education."

Distill all of this information, and what do we know? We as a nation killed forty-five million babies in thirty-one years, it is not in fashion to have more than two children, and if you have more than two children, you must not be very bright.

How does this trend hold up under scrutiny of the scriptures and latter-day prophets? President Ezra Taft Benson said, "I know the special blessings of a large and happy family, for my dear parents had a quiver full of children. Being the oldest of eleven children, I saw the principles of unselfishness, mutual consideration, loyalty to each other, and a host of other virtues developed in a large and wonderful family with my noble mother as the queen of that home.

"Young mothers and fathers, with all my heart I counsel you not to postpone having your children, being co-creators with our Father in Heaven" (Ezra Taft Benson, *Come, Listen to a Prophet's Voice* [Salt Lake City: Deseret Book Company, 1990], 27).

The reasoning of the world excuses every step of the "multiply and replenish" cycle. First: Don't get married until you have experienced the world, received all the education you want, own a home, and have a growing portfolio. Second: Once married, do not rush into parenthood. Wait until you've cemented your relationship and done everything you want to do as a couple. Third: After you've decided that you'd like to try parenthood but quickly realize how difficult and expensive it actually is, have one or two children, put them in daycare and preschool, and as quickly as possible get back into the lifestyle you had B.C. (Before Children). Actually, animals are much more rewarding than children and so much less trouble. Consider a dog or two.

President Benson wrote: "This is the reasoning of the world, and is not pleasing in the sight of God. Mothers who enjoy good health, have your children and have them early. And, husbands, always be considerate of your wives in the bearing of children. Do not curtail the number of your children for personal or selfish reasons. Material possessions, social convenience, and so-called professional advantages are nothing compared to a righteous posterity. In the eternal perspective, children—not possessions, not position, not prestige—are our greatest jewels" (*Come, Listen to a Prophet's Voice*, 27).

Brigham Young said, "There are multitudes of pure and holy spirits waiting to take tabernacles, now what is our duty?—To prepare tabernacles for them; to take a course that will not tend to drive those spirits into the families of the wicked, where they will be trained in wickedness, debauchery, and every species of crime. It is the duty of every righteous man and woman to prepare tabernacles for all the spirits they can" (*Discourses of Brigham Young,* selected and arranged by John A. Widtsoe [Salt Lake City: Deseret Book Company, 1954], 197).

President Spencer W. Kimball put it this way: "When theologians are reeling and stumbling, when lips are pretending and hearts are wandering, and people are 'running to and fro, seeking the word of the Lord and cannot find it'—when clouds of error need dissipating and spiritual darkness needs penetrating and heavens need opening, a little infant is born. Just a few scattered neighbors in a hilly region in the backwoods even know that Lucy is expecting. There is no prenatal care, nor nurses; no hospital, no ambulance, no delivery room. Babies live and die in this rough environment and few know of it.

"Another child for Lucy! No trumpets are sounded; no hourly bulletins posted; no pictures taken; no notice is given; just a few friendly community folk pass the word along. It's a boy! Little do the brothers and sister dream that a prophet is born to them; even his proud parents can little suspect his spectacular destiny. No countryside farmers or loungers at the country store, nor village gossips even surmise how much they could discuss, did they but have the power of prophetic vision.

"'They are naming him Joseph,' it is reported. But not one knows, not even his parents, at this time, that this infant and his father have been named in the scriptures for 3500 years, named for and known to their ancestor Joseph, the savior of Egypt and Israel. Not even his adoring mother realizes, even in her most ambitious dreaming and her silent musings, that this one of her children, like his ancestor, will be the chief sheaf of grain to which all others would lean and the one star to which the sun and moon and the other stars would make obeisance" (*Conference Report,* April 1960, 84).

And as President Benson concluded, "The world teaches birth control. Tragically, many of our sisters subscribe to its pills and practices when they could easily provide earthly tabernacles for more of our Father's children. We know that every spirit assigned to this earth will come, whether through us or someone else. There are couples in the Church who think they are getting along just fine with their limited families but who will someday suffer the pains of remorse when they meet the spirits that might have been part of their posterity. The first commandment given to man was to multiply and replenish the earth with children. That commandment has never been altered, modified, or canceled. The Lord did not say to multiply and replenish the earth if it is convenient, or if you are wealthy, or after you have gotten your schooling, or when there is peace on earth, or until you have four children. The Bible says, 'Lo, children are an heritage of the Lord. . . . Happy is the man that hath his quiver full of them. . .' (Ps. 127:3, 5). We believe God is glorified by having numerous children and a program of perfection for them. So also will God glorify that husband and wife who have a large posterity and who have tried to raise them up in righteousness" (*Conference Report,* April 1969, 12).

The math of the world limits and restricts. The math of heaven multiplies exponentially.

# PELLUCIDITY

The Sunday before general conference, six-year-old John received a handout in Primary that had individual photos of the First Presidency and the Quorum of the Twelve Apostles. His Primary president hoped the children would watch for these prophets, seers, and revelators to speak and that as a result they would get more out of conference.

It worked with John.

As conference began, John carefully cut out each photo, then asked if he could borrow the small light table his mother uses to trace patterns. She helped him set it up and wondered what he would do with it. John watched conference intently. Each time one of the fifteen Apostles began to speak, he put the speaker's photo in the middle of the light table, causing light to beam though and around each photo.

The title of this chapter—"Pellucidity," which is a new word to me—comes from the Latin *pellucidus,* which means "admitting the passage of light, to shine through." The word has probably never been used in exactly this way before, but imagine the spiritual wattage that shines through the Apostles in general conference. The idea creates a beautiful image and challenges each of us to try to live daily life so that the light of Christ can shine through us, radiating His goodness and glory. This is more than a challenge. Christ told His followers: "*Ye* are the light of the world" (Matthew 5:14, emphasis added), meaning when you do as He commands, you become a light table to those with whom you have influence.

In the Sermon on the Mount, Jesus taught His disciples how much light they should radiate. He doesn't want candle-powered believers who hide their limited light under a bushel, only to grow dim and flicker out. He wants believers who radiate a powerful enough light to give "light unto all that are in the house" (Matthew 5:15) and a light located high on a hill that "cannot be hid" (Matthew 5:14). In this dispensation, the Lord told the Saints to "Arise and shine forth, that thy light may be a standard for the nations" (D&C 115:5).

Using the concept of pellucidity, we accept the light of Christ, which cleanses, protects, enlightens, and comforts. We then allow His light to shine through us to help a hurting spouse, a lonely parent, an anxious teen, or a gospel sister who is struggling with testimony, divorce, depression, or death. As disciples of Christ, we can shine our light on family, friends, and neighbors.

One couple recently had an opportunity to use the concept of pellucidity by allowing their light to shine for a stranger. The wife was driving on a treacherous stretch of freeway between two mountains on a winter night with no moon, and her night vision is not perfect. She was traveling under the speed limit, and her squint showed the strain she was feeling. Her husband sat in the passenger seat, wide-eyed. Suddenly, almost simultaneously, they said, "What's that?"

About fifteen feet in front of them, in their lane, was a slow-moving vehicle with no tail lights or brake lights. The wife braked, then moaned as she realized she could have easily hit what appeared to be a long tractor-trailer. She said, "Help me pass him." Her husband thought for a moment, then asked, "What would you think about following him down the canyon to prevent other cars from hitting him?"

As they slowly made their way down the mountain, shielding the slow vehicle from the rear and alerting oncoming drivers to its presence, they realized that what others had done for them throughout their lives was exactly what they were doing for this stranger. They shared memories of times they had been blindly traveling life's dark freeways when someone had shined a guiding and protecting light on them.

From that moment in the premortal council when He accepted His role as Savior, Jesus Christ has been the light, life, and hope of the world. He lights the way through living Apostles and prophets, scripture, priesthood, temple ordinances, bishops, stake presidents, teachers, and our sisters in the gospel. Let's allow His light to shine both through us to others and on us from others as we start and continue the pellucidity cycle.

# DEW FROM HEAVEN

On the first Sunday of each month, fast and testimony meetings take place in more than 23,000 wards and branches throughout the world. Each is a place where testimony, love, and thankfulness are expressed under the influence of the Holy Spirit. A list of those who shared testimony in my ward one Sunday may sound routine, but the gift of the Holy Ghost made this meeting memorable.

- A counselor in the bishopric began by expressing his gratitude for the joy of looking into his parents' eyes at the end of his mission, knowing that he had served faithfully and honorably. He hoped for such a reunion with his heavenly parents someday.
- A Primary teacher shared love for the Savior and for "the best Primary class ever."
- The Primary president spoke of her love for Primary teachers and children and shared her testimony.
- A young father told of his challenge in balancing duties and thanked Heavenly Father for the guidelines inherent in gospel living.
- A nine-year-old girl gave thanks for her wonderful family, especially the blessing of having a father who is deaf.
- A young father wept as he announced his family was moving from the ward. He thanked ward members for teaching him how to be a Christian.
- An eight-year-old boy, a member of the Church for one day, simply testified of the truth of the gospel restored through Joseph Smith.

- An eleven-year-old echoed the same feelings and expressed his gratitude for our prophet.
- A convert of four years told of obstacles and frustrations in her Church activity, but reaffirmed her decision and her testimony of the restoration of the gospel of Jesus Christ.
- A husband whose wife was diagnosed with cancer expressed his love for her, expressed his love for his children, and thanked the members of the ward and Heavenly Father for their many kindnesses.
- A grandfather referred to his experience as a teen in Hitler's youth organization and contrasted that evil regime to the experience of being a member of God's army of men who hold the holy priesthood.
- Another grandfather, breathing oxygen through a tube, thanked the German grandfather for consistently bearing testimony over the many years and credited him with helping to build his own testimony.
- A grandmother told of a disease that is limiting her abilities but expressed gratitude for a priesthood blessing she received to help her continue playing the organ.
- A sensitive closing prayer was said by a young father who just moved his family back to the ward after having grown up here.
- The organist, a man who knows personally the comfort of the Holy Ghost, then played the postlude music, "As the Dew from Heaven Distilling." Even though the words were not being sung, the message somehow seemed to accompany the melody:

> As the dew from heav'n distilling
> Gently on the grass descends
> And revives it, thus fulfilling
> What thy providence intends,
>
> Let thy doctrine, Lord, so gracious,
> Thus descending from above,
> Blest by thee, prove efficacious
> To fulfill thy work of love.

Lord, behold this congregation;
Precious promises fulfill.
From thy holy habitation
Let the dews of life distill. (*Hymns,* 149)

Was this fast and testimony meeting any different from any other? Perhaps not, but at the same time it was extraordinary—for as the dew revives and nourishes each blade of grass individually, the Holy Ghost renews and edifies humble followers of Christ as a congregation. Thus the fitting words in the third verse, "Lord, behold this congregation."

A Christmas song written a few years ago by a man who lives in Seattle explained that there was no need to give him a Christmas present because God had already given him (and everyone else in the Northwest) a generous sign of His love—the many majestic trees that reach heavenward. In a similar way, we don't need presents on Christmas or birthdays because Heavenly Father has given us and continues to bless us with His presence as individuals—"behold, I will tell you in your mind and in your heart, by the Holy Ghost . . ." (D&C 8:2)—and collectively—"For where two or three are gathered together in my name, there am I in the midst of them" (Matthew 18:20).

In the Book of Mormon, we discover that we are not the first people to acknowledge the Holy Ghost as a "most desired" gift. After the crucifixion and resurrection of Jesus Christ, He appeared to the people on what would become known as the American continent. He taught them, healed them, organized His church, and asked them what they desired most from Him. In response, "behold, they knelt . . . and prayed to the Father in the name of Jesus.

"And they did pray for that which they most desired; and they desired that the Holy Ghost should be given unto them" (3 Nephi 19:8–9).

May the Spirit's presence, Heavenly Father's gift to His children, gently distill on you in abundance.

# ANOTHER MARSHMALLOW LESSON

In *Sisters in Zion,* I wrote a chapter titled "Be a Two-Marshmallow Woman" in which I told of an experiment reported by Daniel Goleman in his best-selling book, *Emotional Intelligence.* In the experiment, four-year-old children were taken one at a time into a room where they were told that the experimenter needed to run a quick errand. The experimenter placed one marshmallow on the table and explained to the child that if he could wait to eat the marshmallow until she returned, the child could have two marshmallows. If he could not wait, he could eat the one marshmallow right away.

The experimenter left the room for fifteen to twenty minutes, leaving each child alone. Some children grabbed the marshmallow immediately. Some waited. Through two-way mirrors, the experimenters watched with great interest the children who were delaying gratification. Some of the children covered their eyes so they wouldn't have to stare at temptation. Some talked to themselves, sang, played games with their hands and feet, or tried other ways to distract themselves. Some even tried to go to sleep.

When children who had participated in the initial experiment reached adolescence, they were reevaluated. The children who had resisted the quick marshmallow at age four tended to display similar tratis several years later. Goleman wrote, "Those who had resisted temptation at four were now, as adolescents, more socially competent: personally effective, self-assertive, and better able to cope with the frustrations of life. . . . They were self-reliant and confident, trustworthy and dependable; and they took initiative and plunged into projects. And . . . they were still able to delay gratification in pursuit of their goals" (Daniel P. Goleman, *Emotional Intelligence* [New York: Bantam Books, 1995], 81–82.)

On the other hand, the one-marshmallow adolescents were "more likely to be seen as shying away fr om social contacts; to be stubborn and indecisive; to be easily upset by frustrations; to think of themselves as '*bad*' or unworthy. . . . And, after all those years, they were still unable to put off gratification" (Goleman, 82).

The most amazing statistic came, however, when these same children were reevaluated during their senior year in high school. Goleman summarized, "Those who had waited patiently at four were far superior *as students* to those who had acted on whim. . . . Most astonishingly, they had dramatically higher scores on their SAT tests. The third of children who at four grabbed for the marshmallow most eagerly had an average verbal score of 524 and quantitative (or "math") score of 528; the third who waited longest had average scores of 610 and 652 respectively—a 210-point difference in total score" (Goleman, 82).

Marki Baxter, the Primary president in our ward, did a version of the marshmallow experiment that allowed every child to successfully delay gratification. Even the children who might have snarfed down the one marshmallow didn't, and each got the reward of two marshmallows in the end. Here's how it worked: Marki began talking about how Heavenly Father expects His children to wait for good things to happen as she poured a bag of large marshmallows into a brown paper bag. It took a couple of minutes to get all the marshmallows in the bag, and she talked the entire time.

Then Marki pointed to something in the back of the room. While the children turned to look where she had pointed, Marki switched the bag of big marshmallows for an identical brown paper bag she had hidden in the podium. Then she told the children each of them could take a marshmallow, but they could not eat it. If they waited until she told them they could eat the marshmallow, she said, they'd get a reward.

As the children started taking marshmallows, two things surprised me. First, the marshmallows were miniature marshmallows—not the large ones we had watched Marki pour into the bag. Second, every child seemed to want every other child to get the promised reward. When the first Sunbeam, who didn't understood that he would get something better if he waited, moved the marshmallow toward his mouth, all the other children yelled, "Don't eat it!"

A few children had taken a marshmallow before one of them said, "Hey, you tricked us. They were big marshmallows." When all the children realized there had been a bait and switch, Marki explained that it was a test to see if they could wait for good things to happen. It was so interesting to see how the children responded. Just as in the original experiment, some children reduced temptation by putting the marshmallow on their laps. Some looked away. One put it on his shoe, and another one put it behind his ear.

As the children struggled to delay the gratification of eating the marshmallows, Marki segued into a discussion about prayer. She explained that sometimes Heavenly Father doesn't immediately bless us with everything we pray for. Sometimes we have to wait, and sometimes He says "no." She asked the children why Heavenly Father doesn't simply grant every desire and solve every problem instantly. The children responded with very insightful answers. One said, "Because He knows what's good for us." Another said, "It would be like magic." She helped them understand that if Heavenly Father did everything a person wanted, the person would become lazy and not learn to do things by himself and for himself.

When she was satisfied that the children understood the concept of waiting for blessings, she asked the children why no one had eaten the marshmallows. They all knew! They wanted everyone to get the reward! Marki praised them for caring about each other and likened this to friends and family members helping each other choose the right. Once she felt these two lessons were learned, she took out the original bag of large marshmallows and passed it around. When all the children had received a big marshmallow, she gave them permission to eat both.

It was great to watch the children work together to achieve a common goal. It was also an important reminder for me to watch each child experience the intrinsic benefits of delayed gratification—something we can all strive to experience in mortality.

# TENTACLES OF FAITH, LOVE, AND TESTIMONY

As I was praying about a topic for the monthly ward Relief Society message, the words *before it grows too late* came into my mind. I tried to remember where the words were from for only a minute before it seemed I could hear children's voices singing. I turned in the *Children's Songbook* to the first song, "I Am a Child of God," and scanned the verses.

> I am a child of God,
> And so my needs are great;
> Help me to understand his words
> *Before it grows too late.*
> (*Children's Songbook*, 2; emphasis added)

There in the third verse were the words, "Before it grows too late." Then the question came, "Before it grows too late for what? What is *it?*" The only possible answer comes in the previous line, "Help me *to understand His words.*" Is it ever really too late to understand His words? Probably not, but there is a specific window of opportunity during which we can best teach children—and it is while they are young.

Joseph Smith knew this, and while a prisoner in Liberty Jail he wrote to Emma: "My dear Emma there is great responsibility resting upon you in preserving yourself in honor and sobriety before [our children] and teaching them right things to form their young and tender minds, that they begin in right paths and not get contaminated when young by seeing ungodly examples" (*BYU Studies,* Vol. 13 [1972], 22).

The Doctrine and Covenants states this doctrine as a commandment, and puts squarely on the shoulders of the parents the responsibility for teaching children the gospel before age eight: "And again, inasmuch as parents have children in Zion . . . that teach them not to understand the doctrine of repentance, faith in Christ the Son of the living God, and of baptism and the gift of the Holy Ghost by the laying on of the hands, when eight years old, the sin be upon the heads of the parents. . . .

"And they shall also teach their children to pray, and to walk uprightly before the Lord" (D&C 68:25–28). We have a list! Parents must teach repentance, faith in Christ, baptism, gift of the Holy Ghost, prayer, and general righteous living. Add to that Joseph Smith's counsel: we must be an example as well.

A conversation with a friend showed me the practical aspects of how important it is to teach children while they are young. She told me about the trials they were experiencing with their fifteen-year-old daughter, whom we'll call Ashley. Ashley was becoming increasingly more involved in the sins of the world—daily at her high school and nightly on the Internet. My friend explained that she and her husband were desperately trying to bring Ashley back into the fold. Interestingly, she rebelled at anything they tried that was new—but she accepted as normal whatever was already an integrated part of their family lifestyle. My friend described Ashley as having *selective* rebellion. I asked for some examples.

Every night the family reads from the Book of Mormon before family prayer, something they have done since before Ashley was born. Ashley will take her turn reading a few verses and will also say the prayer.

As another example, the family has had weekly family home evenings since before Ashley was born. Ashley still attends family home evening, participates a little, doesn't spoil it for the younger children, and only complains if it goes on too long.

Since 2001, when Ashley was nine, the family began reading from President Hinckley's book, *Stand a Little Taller,* which provides a thought from him for every day of the year. Before family members go their separate ways in the morning, a parent reads the entry for that day and then prays. Because of a school activity, Ashley leaves before anyone else, but she is still willing to let one of her parents read President Hinckley's advice for the day and listen to her parent pray for her. Every day for six years they have read President Hinckley's words to their children. Can you imagine how this has affected their lives? (I noticed that the initials of *Stand a Little Taller* spell SALT. This book has been as salt to the family, adding spiritual seasoning to each day.)

My friend occasionally allows herself a what-if thought: What if they were just now, when the need is so obvious, trying to implement family prayer or scripture study or family home evening? She likened these established patterns to tentacles of their faith, their love, and their testimonies continually reaching out to Ashley and drawing her in, keeping her close to the family and to the gospel. Her husband feels they are clothing their children with the armor of God, helping them put it on every day until they are able and willing to put it on by themselves.

Sometimes the wrenching ordeal of a wayward child represents total rebellion. President Hinckley counsels: "If any of you have a child or loved one in that condition, do not give up. Pray for them and love them and reach out to them and help them" (Gordon B. Hinckley, *Teachings of Gordon B. Hinckley* [Salt Lake City: Deseret Book Company, 1997], 54). And perhaps all you can do for a season is love and wait. Quoting the Prophet Joseph Smith, Elder Orson F. Whitney said "that the eternal sealings of faithful parents and the divine promises made to them for valiant service in the Cause of Truth, would save not only themselves, but likewise their posterity. Though some of the sheep may wander, the eye of the Shepherd is upon them, and sooner or later they will feel the tentacles of Divine Providence reaching out after them and drawing them back to the fold. Either in this life or the life to come, they will return. They will have to pay their debt to justice; they will suffer for their sins; and may tread a thorny path; but if it leads them at last, like the penitent Prodigal, to a loving and forgiving father's heart and home, the painful experience will not have been in vain. Pray for your careless and disobedient children; hold on to them with your faith. Hope on, trust on, till you see the salvation of God" (*Conference Report,* April 1929, 110).

# THE INCREDIBLES' DNA

Have you seen the blockbuster movie *The Incredibles*? It's my favorite animated movie because the plot hinges on a family that works together. The mother—Mrs. Incredible, also known as Elastigirl—stretches her superhero elastic body to impossible lengths to protect her marriage and children. She is a good role model for today's young women because despite being able to save the world, as superheroes do, she is willing to stay at home and be a mother—a no-nonsense mother who expects her children to obey and help.

When I think of real-life incredible women, one of my heroines is the first woman, Mother Eve, who is the role model of all female role models. From what we know of her, she was as brave as any fictional super hero.

I am thankful for the knowledge and perspective the restored gospel of Jesus Christ gives on Adam and Eve. Other religions see Adam as a follower and Eve as a sinner. But we believe their transgression was a necessary and planned-for part of Heavenly Father's great plan of happiness. I honor Eve for her willingness to make a critical and courageous decision.

The entry for Eve in the *Encyclopedia of Mormonism* reads: "Eve, the first woman of earthly creation, companion of Adam and mother and matriarch of the human race, is honored by Latter-day Saints as one of the most important, righteous, and heroic of all the human family. Eve's supreme gift to mankind, the opportunity of life on the earth, resulted from her choice to become mortal" (Daniel H. Ludlow, ed., *Encyclopedia of Mormonism* [New York: Macmillan Publishing, 1992], 475–476). Modern-day scriptures refer to her as "our glorious Mother

Eve" (D&C 138:39). Understanding genetics as Heavenly Father does, He would have started the human race with His finest.

I became even more interested in Mother Eve when listening to a talk by BYU Professor Scott Woodward, a geneticist who is using his science to do genealogy. If I understand correctly, by identifying a percentage of each of my children's DNA, he will know—not guess—what my DNA is and that of my husband. If he then knows some percentage of my siblings' DNA, he will also know my father's and my mother's DNA. Using this process, Dr. Woodward can go back generation by generation to identify our common ancestors. He says he needs 100,000 samples of DNA to accomplish this.

Dr. Woodward went on to explain that everyone has two parents, which doubles to four grandparents, which doubles to eight great-grandparents, and which continues to double. If you go back 750 years to 1350 A.D., we'd each have a billion potential ancestors. But since there weren't that many people on the earth in 1350 A.D., how does it work? Thirty generations or so ago, everyone was marrying cousins. So as you go back more than thirty generations, most of us have common ancestors. Dr. Woodward said: "Some of us have more common ancestors than others, but the rule is and the law is that as we go back, the numbers increase, yet the number of potential ancestors—or actual ancestors—decreases, and they coalesce" (BYU Family History Fireside, October 11, 2002). Eventually, the number of common ancestors decreases to two—Adam and Eve.

Last year I had another experience with Mother Eve when I vicariously saw her while reading an account from the life of Joseph Smith: "Words of Zebedee Coltrin: Once after returning from a mission to Kirtland, I met Brother Joseph, who asked me if I did not wish to go with him to a conference at New Portage, Ohio. The party consisted of Presidents Joseph Smith, Sidney Rigdon, Oliver Cowdery and me. Next morning at New Portage, I noticed that Joseph seemed to have a far off look in his eyes, or was looking at a distance. Presently he stepped between Brother Cowdery and me, and taking us by the arm said, 'Let's take a walk.'

"We went to a place where there was some beautiful grass, and grapevines and swamp birch interlaced. President Joseph Smith then said, 'Let us pray.'

"We all three prayed in turn—Joseph, Oliver and me. Brother Joseph then said, 'Now brethren, we will see some visions.'

"Joseph lay down on the ground on his back and stretched out his arms, and we laid on them. The heavens gradually opened, and we saw a golden throne, on a circular foundation, and on the throne sat a man and a woman, having white hair and clothed in white garments. Their heads were white as snow, and their faces shone with immortal youth. They were the two most beautiful and perfect specimens of mankind I ever saw. Joseph said, 'They are our first parents, Adam and Eve'" (Larry E. Dahl and Donald Q. Cannon, *Encyclopedia of Joseph Smith's Teachings* [Salt Lake City: Bookcraft, Inc., 1997], 18).

Toward the end of Dr. Woodward's presentation on DNA, a powerful thought hit me: I have some of Eve's DNA! I am literally and actually her daughter! Obviously I realize that every other woman who ever lived on the earth is her daughter as well, but that doesn't change the fact that *I* have some of Mother Eve's DNA. I feel incredibly close to this amazing woman. What a heritage! I am a spirit daughter of God and a physical daughter of Adam and Eve.

Historian Wallace Stegner wrote in the foreword to his book about the Mormon pioneers: "I [do not] doubt their . . . devotion and heroism. . . . Especially their women. Their women were incredible" (Wallace Earle Stegner, *The Gathering of Zion: The Story of the Mormon Trail* [Lincoln, Nebraska: University of Nebraska Press, 1964], 13).

Mother Eve was incredible. Our pioneer sisters were incredible. You and I are incredible when we do what valiant women in every dispensation and every age have done. We, the women of the Church in these latter days, stretch ourselves to impossible lengths and make courageous decisions. *We* could be called *The Incredibles.*

# WHERE DO YOU FIND HAPPINESS?

Elder Jack H. Goaslind gave a talk in April Conference 1986 titled "Happiness." He began: "Last summer I saw an interesting picture as I followed a car on the freeway. It was a large station wagon that had obviously endured many road skirmishes. The top rack was loaded with luggage; the seats were loaded with people. Four bare feet hung out the rear window, and elbows and arms hung out the side windows. In the front seat, the mother was wrestling with a feisty child while simultaneously trying to calm an upset infant. The father was desperately trying to negotiate the heavy traffic. It was obviously vacation time for this family. As I surveyed the situation with some degree of empathy, I noticed a bumper sticker which read, 'Are we having fun yet?'

"I laugh about this scene whenever I recall it. I believe it is amusing because it exhibits a wry insight into human nature. It reveals a very real aspect of the human condition: the largely unfulfilled pursuit of happiness. . . . How many people in this world pursue happiness but find that it eludes them? They contrive pleasures, invent amusements, and invest heavily in recreation. They go abroad in search of this rare gift but fail to see that evidence of it is all around them; the source is within them" ("Happiness," *Ensign,* May 1986, 52).

Disneyland is one such place where people seek happiness. Two of our daughters live near the Magic Kingdom, and we've been lucky enough to go to the park with them many times. While there, I've watched families who have come great distances at substantial expense, hoping for happy family experiences. But all too often, children get tired and parents become frustrated as they try to optimize the opportunity. Those who find happiness at Disneyland realize that it doesn't necessarily come in racing from Dumbo to Buzz Lightyear to the Matterhorn. Instead, it might be found sitting with a three-year-old on a bench watching the ducks swim in the castle's pond or standing in a long line with a teen enjoying the process as much as the event. These people know that pleasures pass, but happiness lasts.

I know many women who are able to recognize happiness. My sister Eileen and her husband, Wayne, are on a mission in Uganda. She writes of the beauty of the people and of the land, and tells how valuable the geckos are because they keep away the snakes. When my in-laws went on a mission, they wrote this about their apartment: "We have two twin beds and a three-drawer chest. In the living room we have a small, square end table and a couch they bought us from D.I. [Deseret Industries Thrift Store]. We scrubbed it for four hours. There is nothing in the kitchen, but when another couple leaves in about two weeks, we'll get their table and chairs. It reminds us of our first apartment in Snowville, Utah, in 1939. We are going to love it here!"

These happy women didn't learn how to find happiness while on their missions. They learned this skill while living their day-to-day lives, and they are actually fulfilling a prophecy given in 1979 by President Spencer W. Kimball. He said, "Much of the major growth that is coming to the Church in the last days will come because many of the good women of the world . . . will be drawn to the Church in large numbers . . . women of the Church are seen as distinct and different—in happy ways—from the women of the world" ("The Role of Righteous Women," *Ensign,* Nov. 1979, 10).

The best part about happiness is that it can be found right here, right now. We don't have to wait until the baby sleeps through the night, until we can take the family to Disneyland, or until everyone is missioned, married, and moved out. Daily happiness is illustrated perfectly with just one example: happiness is smiling at the baby instead of grimacing at the diaper. Happiness for me comes at the end of each day when I kneel and enumerate the day's blessings with Heavenly Father. A happiness shared is a happiness doubled.

One evening Richard and I went to a viewing; our friend's seemingly healthy husband had died playing basketball at age sixty. As we walked into the funeral home, we realized we had arrived late, and family members were preparing to leave; the widow was leaning over the casket in what looked like an intimate moment. We turned to slip away unnoticed when the widow's sister said, "The Linfords are here."

The widow turned to see us, walked over to us, and put her arms around both of us. She said, "Thanks so much for coming. Can you feel the spirit? Isn't it amazing! I've never felt anything like it. I just wish David were here to enjoy it with me."

The truest fact about happiness is that if we can't find it where we are at this moment, we're not likely to find it in the next moment, either. A familiar story tells of a family moving to a new town. They stop at a gas station at the edge of town and ask what kind of people live there. "Well," asks the gas station attendant, "what kind of people live in the town you are moving from?" No matter the answer, the attendant tells them, "You'll find the same kind of people here."

It's the same with finding happiness: it's a state of mind, not a destination.

# WHAT DOES A PROPHET DO WHEN HE'S DEPRESSED?

Moroni, the son of Mormon, is a man of impressive credentials by any standard. He was the last prophet/historian to engrave on the gold plates. With his own hands he buried the future Book of Mormon in the Hill Cumorah. As a glorious resurrected man sent from the presence of God, he tutored the Prophet Joseph Smith for four years before entrusting the plates to Joseph. His coming was foretold in scripture when John the Revelator saw him in vision: "And I saw another angel fly in the midst of heaven, having the everlasting gospel to preach unto them that dwell on the earth, and to every nation, and kindred, and tongue, and people" (Revelation 14:6). Due to his pivotal position in history, Moroni is honored in gold leaf atop temples from Accra, Ghana, to Adelaide, Australia, and from Albuquerque, New Mexico, to Asuncion, Paraguay.

So what did Moroni have to be depressed about?

Turn to Mormon chapter eight. Here we meet Moroni as he finishes his father's record. If we scan the first ten verses, here's what we learn: "Behold I, Moroni . . . have but few things to write . . . after the great and tremendous battle . . . the Nephites . . . were hunted by the Lamanites, until they were all destroyed. . . . my father was also killed by them, and I even remain alone to write the sad tale of the destruction of my people. . . . whether [the Lamanites] will slay me, I know not . . . and whither I go it mattereth not . . ." (verses 1–4).

"I would write . . . if I had room upon the plates, but I have not; and ore I have none, for I am alone. My father hath been slain in battle, and all my kinsfolk, and I have not friends nor whither to go; and how long the Lord will suffer that I may live I know not . . ." (verse 5).

"The Lamanites have hunted my people . . . even until they are no more; and great has been their fall. . . . The Lamanites are at war one with another; and the whole face of this land is one continual round of murder and bloodshed. . . . There are none save it be the Lamanites and robbers that do exist upon the face of the land (verses 7–9).

"And there are none that do know the true God save it be the disciples of Jesus, who did tarry in the land until the wickedness of the people was so great that the Lord would not suffer them to remain . . ." (verse 10).

Moroni's grief for his father, family, and friends—all of whom suffered violent deaths—cannot be measured. He doesn't care where he goes or how long he lives. He feels completely alone and forsaken, but somehow despite all the opposition and personal loss, he conquers his anguish and finishes his father's book. He writes chapters eight and nine of Mormon's book; finds ore and makes new plates; abridges the fifteen chapters of Ether, inserting his own testimony of faith; and adds his own book, containing ten chapters of additional plain and precious doctrines!

How could a man, depressed as he was, not only gird up his loins, but also take fresh courage to such an astonishing degree? As we read from the eighth chapter of Mormon to the end of the Book of Mormon, we see Moroni's pattern for fighting dejection and melancholy with firm resolve:

1. He consciously stops rehearsing his situation: "I make an end of speaking concerning this people" (Mormon 8:13);
2. He remembers who he is and his heritage: "Behold, I am Moroni" (Mormon 8:12); "I am the son of Mormon, and my father was a descendant of Nephi" (Mormon 8:13);
3. He defines himself by his work: "And I am the same who hideth up this record unto the Lord" (Mormon 8:14);
4. He takes courage from others' words—from the Three Nephites: "But behold, my father and I have seen them, and they have ministered unto us" (Mormon 8:11); from his father: "My son, be faithful in Christ" (Moroni 9:25); and from the prophet Ether, whose situation was similar: "Whether the Lord will that I be translated, or that I suffer the will of the

Lord in the flesh, it mattereth not, if it so be that I am saved in the kingdom of God" (Ether 15:34);

5. He forgives and finds purpose. In Moroni 1:1, he says that the Lamanites are trying to kill him, but three verses later he explains that his purpose is to write something that "may be of worth unto my brethren, the Lamanites, in some future day" (Moroni 1:4).
6. He gets to work.
7. He puts his trust in Jesus Christ. In his last words (Moroni 10), he exhorts all to "come unto Christ" (verse 30). He admonishes us to "love God with all your might, mind and strength" (verse 32), to "deny not his power" but be "sanctified in Christ" (verse 33). Then he joyfully bids farewell until "I am brought forth triumphant . . . to meet you before the pleasing bar of the great Jehovah" (verse 34).

When we find ourselves feeling alone and forsaken, do we wallow in self-pity and become increasingly more depressed? Next time you begin that downward spiral, think of Moroni's words and actions, and pull yourself out of it as he did. It's not necessarily easy, but I've tried it with wonderful results. Here are some things to try, following Moroni's pattern:

1. Stop talking about your troubles and woes.
2. Gather courage by remembering your earthly parentage and ancestry. You could write, "I am _____, the daughter of _____." Lift yourself by remembering who you ultimately are—a daughter of God.
3. Define yourself through your work.
4. Gain strength though the words of the prophets, beginning with Adam and continuing through our current prophet, and from family and friends who love you and are positive influences on you.
5. Forgive those who have caused you or your loved ones harm. Forgive yourself, too.
6. Get to work with determination and purpose. As the words fell line by line from Moroni's engraving tool, the momentum

he felt is obvious. He had purpose, determination, courage, and power. It's reminiscent of when President Gordon B. Hinckley was discouraged on his mission and ready to return home. A letter from his father said, "Dear Gordon, I have your recent letter. I have only one suggestion: forget yourself and go to work" (Gordon B. Hinckley, *Faith: The Essence of True Religion* [Salt Lake City: Deseret Book Company, 1989], 115). That same fortitude is described by William Clayton:

> Why should we mourn or think our lot is hard?
> 'Tis not so; all is right.
> Why should we think to earn a great reward
> If we now shun the fight?
> (*Hymns,* 30)

7. Like Moroni, put your trust in Jesus Christ and come unto Him. Love Him with all your might, mind, and strength. Follow His example to help you be a worthy saint. No matter what happens, know that you will ultimately be privileged to meet Moroni and thank him as you stand together to be judged at "the pleasing bar of the great Jehovah" (Moroni 10:34). As William Clayton so eloquently concluded:

> Gird up your loins; fresh courage take.
> Our God will never us forsake;
> And soon we'll have this tale to tell—
> All is well! All is well!
> (*Hymns,* 30)

# EMOTIONAL STRENGTH TRAINING

Do you have daily mood swings? Do you have monthly mood swings? Do you have yearly Seasonal Affective Disorder (SAD)? Some fluctuation in mood is normal and expected; all of us shift between being pretty happy and not too sad (though constant extremes in mood might indicate more serious problems). But maintaining an even mood level often takes concentrated effort. Just as athletes do physical strength training to improve their physical stamina, so emotional strength training is necessary to improve emotional endurance.

The components of emotional strength are hope, optimism, and a good mood. Daniel Goleman, author of *Emotional Intelligence,* explained the importance of hope: "Hope . . . does more than offer a bit of solace amid affliction; it plays a surprisingly potent role in life, offering an advantage in realms as diverse as school achievement and bearing up in onerous jobs. . . . Hope . . . is more than the sunny view that everything will turn out all right. . . . [It's] 'believing you have both the will and the way to accomplish your goals'" (Daniel P. Goleman, *Emotional Intelligence* [New York: Bantam Books, 1995], 87).

My friend just finished her third bachelor's degree. At fifty, she has finally found a career she loves and wants to give her life to—nursing. As part of her wonderful new job, she had to have a tuberculosis test. It was positive, so she was sent to have a chest X-ray. The technician was backed up when she arrived in radiology, so she had about thirty minutes to fret. According to her own report, with every minute she sat waiting she became more convinced that her nursing career was "down the tube." A little voice kept up a constant barrage—"You have tuberculosis. You can't be a nurse. Your career is finished before it's even begun.

You should have stuck with teaching or banking. You were foolish to think you would make a good nurse anyway." She was feeling increasingly pessimistic when she suddenly realized what she was doing to herself.

"Optimists," Dr. Goleman says, "tend to respond actively and hopefully, by formulating a plan of action . . . or seeking out help and advice; they see the setback as something that can be remedied." (Goleman, 88). He wrote that hope and optimism can even predict academic success: "In a study of five hundred members of the incoming freshman class of 1984 at the University of Pennsylvania, the students' scores on a test of optimism were a better predictor of their actual grades freshman year than were their SAT scores or their high-school grades. . . . 'It is the combination of reasonable talent and the ability to keep going in the face of defeat that leads to success. What's missing in tests of ability is motivation. What you need to know about someone is whether they will keep going when things get frustrating. My hunch is that for a given level of intelligence, your actual achievement is a function not just of talent, but also of the capacity to stand defeat'" (Goleman, 88–89).

That's nice rhetoric, but aren't we born optimistic or pessimistic? Is it really possible to change or improve something so basic to personality? Dr. Goleman repeatedly emphasizes that optimism and hope—like helplessness and despair—can be learned. (Yikes—we can learn helplessness and despair, too?)

It would be great if emotional stamina could be bottled and put on a shelf for emergency use—but since it can't, we need to practice hope and optimism every day. How? Just as we physically work out to build stronger muscles or become more flexible, we can do emotional exercises. When you get physically tired of running on a treadmill, you don't stop because you are tired; you keep going a little longer to build your endurance. When you are emotionally tired after being on the hopeful and optimistic treadmill all day, do you give up when the children get home from school because you are tired? No! You push yourself to stay hopeful and optimistic a little longer, and gradually you become emotionally stronger.

My nurse friend's response shows other ways to build emotional strength. She knew about negative voices, and she challenged the pessimism. She knew her probability of having tuberculosis was very low, and she thought rationally about the opportunities before her. Her view of the world went from thinking her nursing career had tanked to expecting good things to happen. When she concentrated on the hopeful and expressed it to herself and to me, her good mood returned.

A list of emotional strength-training exercises might look like this:

1. Push yourself to be a little better every day.
2. Refuse to listen to the negative voice.
3. Challenge pessimism.
4. Expect opportunities.
5. Concentrate on the hopeful.
6. Voice positive, hopeful, optimistic thoughts to yourself and to others.

When hope and optimism become a more permanent part of our personality, the resulting emotional vigor allows us to control mood swings and stay in a good mood. And Dr. Goleman says that the byproduct of being in a good mood is "the ability to think flexibly and with more complexity" (Goleman, 89). The blessing of thinking flexibly is that when obstacles come, the emotionally vigorous person does not withdraw, feel immobilized, or panic, because he or she has learned that obstacles offer opportunity.

Here's an example of how obstacles offer opportunity: A farmer owned an old donkey that fell into the farmer's well one day. Hearing the donkey braying, the farmer rushed over to see what had happened. After assessing the situation, he decided that neither the donkey nor the well was worth the trouble of saving. So he enlisted his neighbors' help to haul dirt to bury the old donkey in the well and put him out of his misery. At first the old donkey was hysterical. But as the farmer and his neighbors continued shoveling and the dirt kept hitting his back, it dawned on him that every time a shovel load of dirt landed on his back, he could shake it off and step up. So that's what he did, blow after blow. Shake it off and step up, shake it off and step up, shake it off and step up. It wasn't long before the old donkey—battered, dirty, and exhausted—stepped triumphantly over the wall of the well. What seemed like it would bury him had actually been the means of his rescue.

It's all in how we handle adversity. No matter how much dirt is thrown on us, let's just shake it off and step up, because obstacles offer opportunities.

# RECEIVING CRITICISM

A mother sat on the piano bench next to twelve-year-old Mariah, helping her practice. Mariah became frustrated and moaned, "All you ever do is criticize me." Mother asked Mariah if she would rather have her mother or her teacher tell her she was forgetting all the B-flats. She asked her to think about the consequences of learning the piece wrong.

Mother then reminded Mariah of an experience at ballet class just a week earlier. Mariah's teacher had positioned her in front of the mirror so she could see how her wrists and elbows looked when rounded in high fifth. After Mariah saw what the position looked like in the mirror, she was able to assume the correct position by herself. Mariah then began to understand that Mother was doing the same thing the ballet teacher had done. She understood that criticism can be a tool to help her improve.

People who understand the potential value of criticism know that criticism is a mirror that helps them see themselves and/or a situation through another's eyes. They respond positively by quickly analyzing the criticism. If it's valid, they thank the person for bringing it to their attention and work on making the suggested change(s). If they feel the criticism is without merit, they forget it, hold no grudge against the critic, and move on.

The Lord uses criticism to help His children. An example of His criticism can be found in scripture: "Yea, the people of Nephi hath he loved, and also hath he chastened them; yea, in the days of their iniquities hath he chastened them because he loveth them" (Helaman 15:3). The Lord chastens because He loves! He is figuratively our mother sitting beside us on the piano bench. He knows our weaknesses and potential. He knows when we need criticism. As Paul said, "Wherefore rebuke them sharply, that they may be sound in the faith" (Titus 1:13). The Lord Himself explains how important it is to accept criticism: "he that will not bear chastisement is not worthy of my kingdom" (D&C 136:31).

Individuals are even criticized by name in scripture. When Sidney Rigdon demonstrated pride, the Lord rebuked him by saying, "I, the Lord, am not pleased with my servant Sidney Rigdon; he . . . received not counsel . . ." (D&C 63:55). When Hiram Page, one of the eight witnesses to the Book of Mormon, was receiving "revelations" that were contrary to the order of the Church, the Lord taught how to give criticism: "thou shalt take thy brother, Hiram Page, between him and thee alone, and tell him that those things which he hath written from that stone are not of me and that Satan deceiveth him" (D&C 28:11).

We know that Heavenly Father often answers prayers through other people, and that at any moment a person may feel prompted to serve us in some timely way. The fulfillment of such a prompting is called a tender mercy—a validation that the Lord is aware of us. Tender mercies usually are thought of as warm and fuzzy mini-miracles. However, God's counsel and chastisement are also tender mercies, and they most often come through other people. I have had this experience, and I am grateful to those who were willing to provide information that caused course corrections in my life. I always hope Proverbs 9:8 describes me: "Rebuke a wise [wo]man, and [s]he will love thee."

It's not always our first instinct to feel grateful when we are criticized, though. Bob and Helen had been out with friends. As they were getting ready for bed that night, Helen matter-of-factly said, "You acted like a fool tonight." Bob felt like he had been shot! His first impulse was to find fault with something Helen had done. His second instinct was one of acting hurt, pouting, or giving her the silent treatment. Then he did a quick rerun of his behavior and realized, "Perhaps she's right." Even though he didn't like the message and knew she could have delivered the criticism in a softer way, his confidence in her made him open to the possibility that her assessment was correct. Her criticism was the catalyst for change and growth, and years later he expressed gratitude for her gumption in stating so clearly how others viewed his actions.

When Richard and I were first married we had some wonderful friends whom I'll call Brian and Sue. One night we were out together and, as I did in those days, I corrected Richard when he said something cost $20 when it was actually $22. Brian immediately said to me, "You are always correcting him. He was close enough. It doesn't matter, and we don't care." How right he was! Without Brian's pointed rebuke I don't know when or if I would have learned how much I was damaging my marriage.

If the purpose of criticism is to affect change, the criticizer should deliver the message with tact and care instead of blurting it out in a frustrating moment. More criticism would be accepted and used if it were presented in the best possible way—given at the optimum moment, sandwiched between two slices of praise, artfully mentioned in casual conversation, or appropriately delivered behind closed doors. But even a clumsy delivery does not invalidate valuable criticism. Bob's chastisement by Helen and my chastisement by Brian weren't gentle, but they were too beneficial to disregard because of presentation.

I always loved my father's response to correction when he made an inaccurate judgment or misunderstood something. When he realized his error, he'd say, "I stand corrected." There was no defensive excusing himself, no counter-criticizing, no sulking, no shifting the blame to someone else. He was wise. I hope I can be like him and view criticism as an important tool in self-improvement. I hope I will always thank the person sitting beside me on the piano bench.

# SHAPING BEHAVIOR

Shaping is a training technique that molds behavior with the philosophy that behavior that gets noticed gets repeated and that voluntary actions are affected by what happens immediately after an act. For example, when your child gets close to a desired behavior, you give reinforcement to help your child understand—sometimes at a subconscious level—what is desirable. Shaping is based on the premise that human behavior can be directed much as a potter molds a mound of clay.

Here's an example of how it works. When your child first dresses himself, you praise his effort even if his pants are on inside out and his shoes are on the wrong feet. As you subsequently teach and your child becomes more proficient, you praise not the fact that he dressed himself, but that he put his pants on correctly. When he learns which shoe goes on which foot, he receives more praise. Shaping doesn't demand that your child dress himself completely and perfectly before you give him any praise. It rewards your child's current level of expertise and allows him to learn a skill in increments.

Shaping indirectly teaches both you and your child to watch for the positive rather than negative. You praise him for what he does right rather than reminding, chiding, or demanding that he achieve a level of fluency or expertise that his age, maturity, or talents don't allow. After a single family home evening on being polite, you don't expect your child to be perfectly polite in every setting from that day on. Politeness, which is only one example, is taught repeatedly at various ages, stages, and settings based on the child's awareness and social acumen.

An important part of shaping is to clearly define what's expected. Let's say you ask your child to clean his room. What *clean* means to you and what *clean* means to him may be worlds apart. But when you specify with an age-appropriate list of what constitutes a clean room, you and your child are working with the same definition. To a nine-year-old you might say, "Please clean your room by hanging up the clothes that go in the closet, by folding away those that belong in the drawers, and by putting the ones that are dirty in the hamper. Then straighten the books on your bookshelf and vacuum your carpet."

If you define, as a component of polite behavior, that your child should greet guests by name who come to your home, it takes more than saying, "Be polite when guests come to the door." Your child may not understand *polite* and he can't be expected to know what being polite is unless you teach him. Imagine that your ten-year-old son answers the door when your visiting teachers come. After they leave, you pat him on the back and say, "Dan, you greeted Sister Clark and Sister Smith so nicely. You called them by name and invited them to come in. You were very polite. Next time, you might also ask them to sit down." In this example, you affirmed his polite behavior and added another element to the definition of what it means to be polite.

Unfortunately, *shaping* is both wonderful and frightening. Shaping is *wonderful* because when appropriately used, it can positively change and improve behavior. But it is *frightening* because it occurs every day in every interaction whether you know it or not. Without purposeful, planned shaping, it happens by default—and it can actually reinforce negative behavior.

A mother may teach her child to respect her elders. But when she tries to get a laugh by telling about something rude the child did or said, she unwittingly "shapes" her child's behavior in the opposite direction. The same default shaping occurs when a parent repeats those "cute" comments toddlers make about bodily functions. As the child gets older and continues to make such comments, the parent becomes aghast and chastises him for being rude or crude. Imagine how confusing that is for the child. A parent might teach and encourage a child to respect his physical body as the temple it is, but without shaping that behavior through good example in word and deed, a parent shapes undesirable behavior by default.

You've heard the saying, "You catch more flies with honey than with vinegar." That's how intentional shaping works. Shaping is honey. Vinegar is the set of negative disciplining techniques parents use, such as criticizing, yelling, insulting, threatening, coercing, and being sarcastic. Parents use these negative techniques because they don't know how to parent in any other way. But there is another way: the shaping way, in which we positively and patiently teach in increments—a little here, a little there, some today, more tomorrow. It's similar to one way Heavenly Father parents: "For behold, thus saith the Lord God: I will give unto the children of men line upon line, precept upon precept, here a little and there a little; and blessed are those who hearken unto my precepts, and lend an ear unto my counsel, for they shall learn wisdom; for unto him that receiveth I will give more" (2 Nephi 28:30).

As mentioned, shaping molds behavior much as a potter sculpts clay. For all of us, that similarity has great significance: "But now, O LORD, thou *art* our father; we *are* the clay, and thou our potter; and we all *are* the work of thy hand" (Isaiah 64:8).

# THE ABSOLUTE CURE FOR SIBLING RIVALRY

A parenting "expert" on a television interview had a thesis that startled me. She said the absolute cure for sibling rivalry was to have only one child! She was serious, and said there is actually a name for these families: *singletons*. Is being part of this growing singleton group the only way to prevent sibling rivalry? If you have a sibling, is there always rivalry? The answer to both is no.

Instead of limiting the number of children to one, let's consider five good parenting techniques that help minimize the negative aspects of sibling rivalry and encourage positive sibling interactions.

1. Many believe the world is a place of scarce resources. The scarcity mentality says that if you have more, I have less, because there's only so much to go around. That mindset can spill over into families, where children may believe there's "not enough"—time, love, money, or whatever else—to go around. The best way to counteract the resulting selfishness and competitiveness is to model and teach gratitude.

Model gratitude by expressing specific thanks to Heavenly Father in prayer, by verbally telling others how grateful you are for them, by showing appreciation for your possessions, and by sharing. Children learn gratitude as they see that their parents govern their desires for material possessions. You've heard it said, "You can never get enough of what you don't need." Children learn gratitude for nature when their parents preserve and protect living things. They also learn gratitude when they are taught to respect others' time and energy. If you model an attitude of scarcity, there will always seem to be a short supply of attention, love, and approval. The focus will be on what you don't have, what you didn't get, and who got more. If you model an outlook of plenty, thankfulness will be the result. Your children will be grateful for what they have instead of dwelling on what they lack.

2. Parents unwittingly generate competition between siblings by emphasizing differences—who's the tallest, the fastest, the smartest, the best in school, and so on. Parents should resist making comparisons by creating an atmosphere in which children ask themselves *Am I doing my best?* instead of *Am I doing better than my sibling?* This is accomplished by helping children feel that when one of them succeeds, the entire family succeeds. Comparisons may stimulate some personalities to greater achievement, but at what cost? Will the child feel his value hinges on continually doing better than someone else? Comparisons may cause other personalities to give up because they feel the bar is set too high. Parents can model healthy competition by the way they interact with their own siblings, peers, and with each other.

3. A third way to decrease sibling rivalry is to create an environment in which every child is parented as an individual. This idea came from Mother Teresa, who served in India for many years. According to tradition, she felt inadequate when she arrived in India because the needs were too great; she was just one small woman—how could she combat the rampant disease and lack of education among the masses? She prayed to be transferred somewhere less formidable when a voice said to her, "Minister to the one nearest to you." (*Ministering* means attending to needs.) So she got to work, caring for the one nearest to her.

How does a mother minister? She comforts, teaches, hugs, and praises each child, one by one. When my daughter Christine calls from her home in Maryland, she says, "Hi, Mom, it's your favorite daughter." And she's right. At that moment, she is the one nearest to me, the only one I can minister to at that moment. How does this work with young children? Imagine Jacob is playing quietly beside you on the porch and Nathan is riding his bike in the driveway. Jacob is the only one with whom you can interact at the moment, so you talk and share and show interest and concern in Jacob. But then you hear a scream and see that Nathan has fallen, so you go to him and attend to his needs, cleaning and doctoring his physical and emotional wounds. This is how the Savior ministered: "and he took their little children, one by one, and blessed them, and prayed unto the Father for them" (3 Nephi 17:21).

4. Some parenting books advise parents to let their children argue with each other because it teaches them to resolve their own problems. Other books suggest that parents should get involved in every squabble, acting as judge and jury. King Benjamin suggests a third approach: "And ye will not suffer your children that they go hungry, or naked; neither will ye suffer that they transgress the laws of God, and fight and quarrel one with another, and serve the devil, who is the master of sin, or who is the evil spirit which hath been spoken of by our fathers, he being an enemy to all righteousness.

"But ye will teach them to walk in the ways of truth and soberness; ye will teach them to love one another, and to serve one another" (Mosiah 4:14–15). Teach your children in a spirit of love and gratitude to serve each other, to be aware of needs, to speak kindly, to show affection, and to resolve differences without quarreling.

5. Life isn't fair—and when parents try to make it fair they actually increase sibling rivalry. For example, if Parker needs a pair of new shoes, Tyler doesn't get a pair of new shoes (or something else of equal value). Instead, Tyler is taught to be happy that Parker has new shoes. When a child receives a compliment, the parent doesn't compliment the other children who are present—because if everyone is complimented, no one is complimented. Teach children that they will experience greater happiness when they freely praise one another and when they are happy for each other's successes or possessions.

Instead of seeing sibling rivalry as an unsolvable problem—and certainly instead of "fixing" the problem by having only one child—let's help our children enjoy each other, learn from each other, be grateful for each other, and serve one another. Let's help them understand that life can never be fair, but that it can be enjoyable and rewarding as we choose to make it so. Let's teach our children sibling empathy—to rejoice in their siblings' successes and feel sad with them in their setbacks. As the inevitable problems arise, let's help our children see the beneficial aspects of being a family and help them enjoy the fact that they are going to be siblings for a very long time.

# MARITAL GARBAGE CANS

A middle-aged couple on the farm had a . . . quarrel at breakfast time. Later in the day they started for town in the buggy with a fine team of horses to sell their vegetables and eggs. As the horses trotted along, Mary said, 'John, why can't we travel together like these horses do? They don't quarrel and fight.' John said, 'Mary, we could if there was only one tongue between us'" (Hugh B. Brown, *Conference Report,* October 1954, 16).

The tongue on a horse-drawn carriage is the harnessing pole that attaches to the front axle. There is only one. But as humans, each of us comes equipped with a tongue. So since having one tongue between them is not physically possible, how can a couple harness their tongues?

There is no other skill as necessary to peacefully resolving differences in marriage as the wise use of the tongue, and so it has been since the beginning of marriage. Adam and Eve's peaceful life in the Garden of Eden was disrupted when Eve made a unilateral decision and ate the forbidden fruit. Many problems in marriage occur when one marriage partner makes a significant decision without consulting the other. After Adam realized that Eve would be cast out of the Garden, he must have struggled with his decision to obey one of God's commandments and be alone in the Garden or to keep the other commandments and be expelled from the Garden with Eve. No compromise was possible. Can you hear the conversation? Adam made clear his point of view; Eve explained hers. They might have gone back and forth for hours, or perhaps days. But finally Adam said, "Eve, I've given this some serious thought, and you are right. Let me have a bite of that fruit."

Do you think that as they came to a unity of purpose Adam called Eve names? Do you think that Eve criticized Adam or made accusations against him? Do you think one or the other lost control and said hurtful things? Do you think either of them swore? Do you think they complained to God about how difficult it was to deal with the other? Did they murmur? I can't imagine that they did anything but reason together in love.

Living in the intimate relationship of marriage can bring out the worst. It's so easy to fall into patterns where unkind, impatient, irritated-sounding words are tossed back and forth. It's easy to chide, rebuke, blame, and scold. It's easy in moments of frustration when plans are changed or aborted to be petty or to dredge up the past or to pour salt in sensitive wounds. Negativity comes with all of the above.

Living in the intimate relationship of marriage can also bring out the best. In marriage we can truly learn to empathize, understand, and feel our spouse's emotions and motives. Our words can be positive and filled with faith and hope. We can remember to say *please* and *thank you*, no matter how long we've been married. We can exercise restraint, give compliments, and pray for the language of angels to give expression to our sentiments of love. We can show respect by being quiet and allowing our spouse uninterrupted time to talk. We can admit when we're wrong and quickly and freely say, "I'm sorry." We can ask one of the best questions in the world: "What may I do to help?"

A friend told me of an upsetting argument she had with her husband. As the day wore on, she began to feel worse and worse about what she had said. Then she recalled an old family home evening lesson about putting bad words in a garbage can. She felt the need for a marital garbage can where she could figuratively toss unkind and unnecessary words instead of tossing them at her husband. She happened to have a small, decorative garbage can, so she wrote the following poem, taped it to the garbage can, and gave it to her husband:

I give to you this garbage can
A small symbolic gift
To bring back happy feelings
'Cause our marriage has a rift.

I'm sorry for my unkind words
I know I criticized.
Forgive me for my pettiness
I want to empathize.

I'll try to never dredge up or
Recycle past bad things,
I'll emphasize the positive,
Discarding murmurings.

I know my hasty, thoughtless words
Did lash and wound your soul.
I'm sorry for the putdowns that I
Scolded, lost control.

I do respect and love you
It was really all my fault;
I opened up a fest'ring wound
And in it poured some salt.

I should have listened to you,
Praying for the Spirit's peace.
I know that if I'll do these things
We'll watch our love increase.

Harnessing horses to a carriage demands proper use of the tongue; without it, nothing works as it should. Being happily harnessed in marriage is all about bridling our verbal exchanges. It's all about how we use the tongue.

# ASSUMING GOOD MOTIVE

When I was eleven, I walked home from school feeling sick. As I arrived home, I realized it was Wednesday—Primary day. I knew I had to get to the meetinghouse because my mother, the Primary president, would worry and come looking for me if I didn't show up. So I set out for the meetinghouse. But with every step I felt progressively sicker. It hurt to swallow. My legs felt rubbery, and I knew I had a fever.

Arriving at the meetinghouse, I slumped into my seat as the opening song was being sung. I tried to get my mother's attention, but she was occupied helping a younger child get ready to say the opening prayer. As another song began, I was startled when the Primary chorister shoved her songbook in my face with a glare that commanded I join in the song. She assumed I was being rebellious and refusing to sing.

Assumptions can be risky. A woman and her twin brother were at a restaurant celebrating their fortieth birthdays. Both are beautiful, with dark hair and eyes and striking features. As they were laughing and enjoying their time together over lunch, the woman felt someone watching her. She glanced up to see a fellow Relief Society sister looking at her with a shocked expression on her face. She quickly realized that her ward friend, who didn't know she was a twin, thought she was out with a handsome man who was not her husband.

A similar situation happened one day when a woman called a restaurant to order takeout. When she arrived, she was told to pick up the food in the restaurant's bar. Sure enough, as she sat at the bar waiting for her order, two acquaintances came into the restaurant and saw her there.

How often do we misjudge situations and motives? A car suddenly stops in front of us for no apparent reason; a child's coach pulls him out of a game; a friend doesn't show up for an appointment; someone in a class we are teaching acts bored or falls asleep; the week after you wear a new sweater to church another sister shows up with one just like it.

Jumping to conclusions and reacting with negative assessments can become a habitual way of looking at the world. A solution to this negative, fault-finding, accusatory style of responding to life is to assume the other person had a good motive for acting the way he or she did. If the Primary chorister from my youth had assumed good motive, she would have remembered that I did not usually misbehave. She would have excused my apparent lack of interest in singing that day by thinking, "She's usually not like this; something must be wrong. I wonder if she's ill?"

Even if we focus on correcting this kind of thinking, others may not. If we are on the suspicious side of a situation, then it's smart to quickly clear up any question. When the woman having lunch with her twin saw the look on her ward member's face, she immediately went to her and said, "Come and meet my twin brother."

There will always be problems with judging accurately and with responding in an appropriate way. Humans have only two eyes with which to view a situation. Perspective makes all the difference. As an example of how it works, think of a basketball game from the vantage point of the coach, from the view of a player who never gets off the bench, from the perspective of the star player, from the outlook of a cheerleader, from the view of a student too shy to go to a game, from the experience of a member of the band, from the standpoint of the last player cut from the team, from the viewpoint of a player's parent, and from the view of the custodian.

Brigham Young said, "Judge not each other rashly, for you will find that ninety-nine wrongs out of a hundred committed by men are done more in ignorance than from a design to do wrong" (*Journal of Discourses,* 10:232).

I try to remind myself to leave the judging to the only Person who has a three-hundred-sixty-degree view: our Father in Heaven. The Savior said, "Judge not, that ye be not judged.

"For with what judgment ye judge, ye shall be judged; and with what measure ye mete, it shall be measured to you again" (Matthew 7:1–2).

Let's be patient in judgment; wait for the facts; see the *why* behind the actions; assume good motive; find the positive. When we do judge inappropriately, let's apologize quickly and judge as we would like to be judged.

# BLESSINGS FOR NON-GOSSIPERS

My former Relief Society president, Carol, told a story about Becky, her son's pet boa constrictor that lived in her basement for many years. She described the day her daughter took Becky to show-and-tell, grabbed Becky the wrong way, and got bitten. Carol explained that a snake's bite inflicts painful wounds that can be sore for a couple of weeks, just like gossip. But unlike snake bites that heal, some gossip bites fester forever. As stated in the scriptures, "The words of a talebearer are as wounds, and they go down into the innermost parts of the belly" (Proverbs 18:8).

Each of us quietly bears a painful sorrow, a problem, or a burden, and every person makes mistakes. I wish I could erase certain aspects of my past, as I assume you do. Instead of helping us overcome errors of the past, gossip often brings the past to the present, creating fresh wounds and additional sorrow. It causes division and creates distrust. It harms individual reputations and destroys corporate empires. It doesn't allow for repentance, restitution, or forgiveness.

Gossip involves talking about others, whether the information is true or false. "Too many people seem to think that it is only gossip if it is unsubstantiated rumor. But something may be completely true and still be no one else's business. Truth does not justify gossip any more than need justifies theft. And to excuse gossip by saying that it is common knowledge is similar to justifying sin because 'others are doing it' . . . (Larry Hiller, "On Keeping Confidences," *Ensign,* June 1985, 25). Richard L. Evans said, "If it hurts a person or you cannot (would not of courtesy) ask them face to face, then you shouldn't talk to others about it."

Many mothers have counseled their children, "Those who tell tales say more about themselves than they do about those of whom they speak." What do we reveal about ourselves if we gossip?

1. We demonstrate that we can't be trusted. If I share gossip with you, will I gossip about you when you're not around?
2. We advertise that we focus on the negative.
3. When we gossip, it's like saying, "I'm selfish. I want to take your time. I want to be the center of attention. I am gossiping so you will focus on me."
4. When we gossip, we show that the words of the Lord are not efficacious in our life. The Lord advises: "And see that there is no iniquity in the church, neither hardness with each other, neither lying, backbiting, nor evil speaking" (D&C 20:54).

There are no better words written about governing what we say than those written in James 3:1–18. James says that if you can control your tongue, you are "able also to bridle the whole body" (verse 2). He gives the example of putting "bits in the horses' mouths, that they may obey us; and we turn about their whole body" (verse 3). He likens the tongue to "a very small helm" that turns about great ships (verse 4). He uses fire as an image: "Even so the tongue is a little member, and boasteth great things. Behold, how great a matter a little fire kindleth!" (verse 5). He compares the tongue to poison: "But the tongue . . . is an unruly evil, full of deadly poison" (verse 8). James asks how blessings and cursings can come out of the same mouth, then says, "My [sisters], these things ought not so to be" (verse 10). "Doth a fountain send forth at the same place sweet water and bitter?" (verse 11). Finally, James summarizes: "If any [wo]man among you seem to be religious, and bridleth not [her] tongue, but deceiveth [her] own heart, this [wo]man's religion is vain" (James 1:26).

So no matter what the excuse is for gossiping, let's take James's advice that "these things ought not to be." Let's not tell tales or reveal secrets. Let's remember: "Once something is made public, it cannot be recalled. And when information is wrongfully used, deep harm can be done to individuals and institutions. So much strife and discontent can be avoided when we learn to keep confidences. 'Where no wood is, there the fire goeth out: so where there is no talebearer, the strife ceaseth.' (Prov. 26:20)" (Larry Hiller, "On Keeping Confidences," 25).

Boa constrictors bite, but you and I can choose not to gossip bite. Let's become a pure fountain, "full of charity towards all men. . . ." As we don't speak or even think gossip, we will come closer to the goal of having virtue garnish our thoughts unceasingly (see D&C 121:45).

Incredible blessings await when we choose not to gossip.

1. As we demonstrate charity by not gossiping, "then shall thy confidence wax strong in the presence of God" (D&C 121:45).
2. When we don't gossip, we receive the Holy Ghost as our "constant companion" (D&C 121:46).
3. Others will trust us and share confidences with us because they know we will not repeat those confidences. Strong, loving relationships come to those who keep confidences.
4. The quiet, unspoken love we demonstrate by not starting or passing on gossip will be noticed by the Lord, and blessings will follow. "I, the Lord, am bound when ye do what I say" (D&C 82:10).

Let's refrain from gossiping and lay claim to these incredible blessings.

# IS FAILURE THE ENEMY OF SUCCESS?

Arthur Gordon's *A Touch of Wonder* (Jove, 1974) is subtitled, "An Invitation to Fall in Love with Life" and bursts with beautiful, uplifting stories and ideas. Surprisingly, a recurrent theme of the book is failure. What could be beautiful and uplifting about failure?

Mr. Gordon tells the story of leaving his native Georgia as a young man with a dream of becoming a great writer in New York City. After a year of rejection slips, he stumbled into an accidental, fortuitous interview with Thomas Watson, who was president of the most successful company in the world at that time—IBM. After a few minutes together, Mr. Watson was so impressed with this innocent and promising young man that he took him to lunch and offered him a job.

"Thank you, sir," Gordon said, "but machines don't like me. What I want to be eventually is. . . ." He stopped, afraid to reveal his true ambition. Deciding, however, that he couldn't lie to such an insightful person, he told Mr. Watson about the year of writing failures.

Mr. Watson leaned back in his chair and said, "Would you like me to give you a formula for writing success? . . . It's quite simple, really. Double your rate of failure. . . .

"You're making a common mistake. . . . You're thinking of failure as the enemy of success. But it isn't at all. Failure is a teacher—a harsh one, perhaps, but the best. You say you have a desk full of rejected manuscripts? That's great! Every one of those manuscripts was rejected for a reason. Have you pulled them to pieces looking for that reason? That's what I have to do when an idea backfires or a sales program fails. You've got to put failure to work for you. . . .

"You can be discouraged by failure—or you can learn from it. So go ahead and make mistakes. Make all you can. Because, remember, that's where you'll find success. On the far side of failure" (Arthur Gordon, *A Touch of Wonder* [Jove Publishing, 1974], 66–67).

Arthur's attitude changed when he heard that advice. Did yours? Mine did. When things don't go right or when I achieve less than I hoped for, I sometimes do feel I've failed. According to Thomas Watson, failing doesn't make you a failure—instead, you've discovered one way something won't work. Failing is a discovery process and can be a solid stepping stone, much like rungs on a ladder. We fail only when we stop trying. If nine out of ten things fail, we must courageously try ten more things.

In another anecdote about failure, one of Thomas Watson's employees made a $10 million mistake. Knowing he was finished at IBM, the employee took his letter of resignation to Mr. Watson. Mr. Watson looked at the letter and then at the employee and said, "Do you think I would let you leave now? I've just spent ten million dollars training you!"

Another Thomas—Thomas Edison—had an amazing ability to persist through failure. After publicly announcing that he would invent a lighting device that would replace the gas lamp, he failed in more than ten thousand different experiments. But because he persevered, history books now record that Thomas Edison invented the first incandescent light bulb on October 21, 1879.

One way to find success is to participate with others toward achieving common goals. When you help someone achieve success, you share in that success, and you celebrate together. If you work together and an effort fails, you don't have to bear the weight of the loss alone. In human dynamics, it's like mutual funds, sharing and equalizing the gains and losses.

A well-known community leader, successful by every standard, made a list when he was twenty-one of fifty things he was going to accomplish in life. About half of them were things over which he had control—get married, earn a Ph.D., write a book, travel to specific destinations, learn to skydive. He has achieved almost all of those goals. But though he is highly motivated to achieve every goal, he cannot accomplish those goals over which he has no control—no matter how much he labors, sweats, and stays focused. Consequently, some goals—such as becoming a United States senator and being the father of twelve children—are unfulfilled dreams. Is he a success or a failure? Thomas Watson would say he's a success.

That's just how life is. We set goals and get to work. Then the realities of the process begin to challenge our grit; it's harder than we anticipated. There are unforeseen obstacles. We run into hurdles. Some we get over, but some trip us or knock us down. Our challenge is to get back up and try to overcome the same obstacle again—to go around it, over it, through it, or change to a different track with different hurdles. We can embrace our failures because they often become eventual stepping stones to success.

# SOMETHING TO LAUGH ABOUT

Laughter isn't something usually associated with the temple, and I didn't laugh at the time, but funny things do happen in the Salt Lake Temple, where I serve as an ordinance worker. I remember one of them with real fondness.

As you know, the ways of the temple are very specific, and everything has to be done correctly. These "temple ways" are clearly explained in a letter each couple receives after making an appointment to be married. One of the instructions states that formal attire—such as tuxedos and bridesmaid gowns—is not appropriate dress for guests attending the ceremony.

One morning I was assigned as coordinator in the bride's room when I received a call from one of the assistant matrons. She told me a bride's mother had shown up in a formal gown and she asked me to "handle" the situation—which meant I needed to ask the mother to change into a temple dress. I said a little prayer, asking for the right words to help the mother understand that temple procedures are strict because the temple is the house of the Lord, and that it's all about His ways, not our ways. Then I went to find this mother. I introduced myself and very gently told her the policy on formal wear, explained that the policy was detailed in the letter her daughter received, and asked her to please change into a white temple dress.

Her answer was not what I'd hoped. She said she was not changing into a white temple dress because she wanted her daughter to be the only person in white. I smiled and said, "Okay, what are the other options?" Trying to calm her mother, the bride said, "Mom, why don't you wear my skirt and tee with your jacket?" Then, looking at me, she asked, "Would that be all right?" I was very relieved to have a solution, said I thought that would be wonderful, and then left to attend to some other brides as mother and daughter went to make the change.

A few minutes later the mother saw me and said, "I think this will work, but I need a pair of pantyhose." I hadn't noticed that she had worn sandals with bare legs. "No problem," I said. "I'll go to the clothing desk and get a pair of white pantyhose."

When I asked for the pantyhose, the clothing workers looked at me in astonishment. One of them said, "We haven't done pantyhose for years. We only have knee-highs." Knee-highs wouldn't work, because the daughter's skirt hit just above the middle of the mother's knees, which would leave two to three inches of bare knee between the skirt and the knee-high.

I went back and reported to the mother and bride. They looked at me with despair, wondering how to resolve the situation, when I had an idea. "Don't lose hope," I said. "I think I have an extra pair of pantyhose in my locker. I'll go check." I ran to my locker and looked. No pantyhose. I grabbed a pair of white knee-highs and returned to the bride and mother.

"This is the grossest thing I've ever offered anyone in my life, but if you'd like, you can have the pantyhose I'm wearing," I said. Without a second of hesitation the mother clapped her hands and said, "Done!" and extended her hand to take them from me. I went into the locker next to hers, took off my pantyhose, shook them a little to cool them down (I *had* been running all over the temple), and handed them over the locker to her. As they left for the sealing room, the mother gave me a hug, and I whispered, "You know I don't want them back, don't you?" She laughed and nodded, and they were on their way!

A lot of research suggests that laughter truly is the best medicine. "A belly laugh may be as good for the heart as a vigorous workout, according to Michael Miller, M.D., of the University of Maryland Medical Center. Miller showed funny scenes from the movie *King Pin* and grimmer ones from *Saving Private Ryan* to 20 volunteers. For up to 45 minutes after viewing the comedy, the viewers' arteries were relaxed, and their blood flowed more freely; but after the war movie, their artery walls tensed up, restricting blood flow. 'Thirty minutes of exercise three times a week and 15 minutes of hearty laughter each day should be part of a healthy lifestyle,' Miller told the American College of Cardiology on March 14, 2005" (*Vegetarian Times,* June 2005). There is actually an organization—The Association for Applied and Therapeutic Humor—whose mission is to "To advance the understanding and application of humor and laughter for their positive benefits."

Another incentive to laugh more: "Laughter burns calories, according to recent research, and a daily laughter workout of 15 minutes can burn 40 calories and melt away 4 pounds over the course of a year. No kidding. The scientific evidence comes from researchers who calculated the average energy expenditure of laughter to be 0.099 kcal/min" (Sally Koch Kubetin and Jane Salodof MacNeil, *Internal Medicine News,* February 15, 2005, 82–83).

Daniel Goleman wrote: "The intellectual benefits of a good laugh are most striking when it comes to solving a problem that demands a creative solution. One study found that people who had just watched a video of television bloopers were better at solving a puzzle long used by psychologists to test creative thinking" (Daniel P. Goleman, *Emotional Intelligence* [New York: Bantam Books, 1995], 85).

The average adult laughs fifteen times a day. When you laugh, others laugh, making it the best contagious disease. According to howstuffworks.com, researchers suggest that "humans have a 'detector' that responds to laughter by triggering other neural circuits in the brain, which, in turn, generates more laughter." At worldlaughtertour.com you can listen to eight different laughs, ranging from a baby's giggle to a hearty ho-ho-ho—and you'll most likely laugh at the laughs. (Go to "Fun Stuff" under "Links" to hear the laughs.)

And have you ever noticed that things seem funnier when you're with others? It's not at all surprising that people laugh more when they in a group than when they are alone. Here's what the experts say: "People are 30 times more likely to laugh in social settings than when they are alone (and without pseudo-social stimuli like television). Even nitrous oxide, or laughing gas, loses much of its oomph when taken in solitude . . ." (howstuffworks.com).

Laughter sounds like the best thing ever. Is laughter ever wrong? As with everything good, there is a counterfeit. Loud or excessive laughter (see D&C 88:69) that is a result of ill temper, that is in response to sordid subjects, that is part of drunken or crude behavior, or that makes light of the misfortunes of others is not healthful or Christ-like. True humor comes with joy and delight and is intelligent and clean.

Good-natured laughing is good for the health and the psyche. Laughter alters moods by bringing cheer and eases tension by creating calm. Humor is most important in the home and with family because the closer in proximity humans live, the more they can irritate each other. That's why there's a need for good humor and lots of it.

If you made a list of the people you most enjoy being around, it is almost guaranteed that every person on your list would be someone who enjoys life, smiles, and laughs. If your friends made such a list, would your name be on it?

Histories of Abraham Lincoln report he suffered with the tendency for melancholy and depression all his life, but that he countered this disposition with humor. According to abilitymagazine.com, Lincoln loved to laugh. "His closet and dearest friends spoke of his jovial demeanor. . . [and his] mirthful and animated expression. . . . His storytelling was underscored with his own laughter, and he was known to often double up before he could get to the punch line of the story."

President Lincoln had the gift to see humor in the everyday, a significant fact because he experienced great personal loss—the death of a newborn brother when he was three; the death of his mother, aunt, and uncle when he was nine; the passing of his sister when he was eighteen; the death of his alleged sweetheart Ann Rutledge; and the deaths of two of his sons. He also lived with an unhappy wife. Through all this, he found humor in the routine. For example, Lincoln was walking down a dimly lit stairway in the War Department building at some point during the Civil War. A young officer who was carrying important papers rushed up the same stairway and crashed head-on into the president. "Ten thousand pardons!" the officer gasped. "One is enough," said President Lincoln. "I wish the whole army could charge like that."

Even if we are prone to melancholy, even if we are asked to change out of our beautiful gown and wear warm secondhand pantyhose, let's try smiling, laughing, and finding humor in daily life.

# HOW GOOD IS YOUR MEMORY?

Have you heard the story about the two women who had been friends for more than seventy years? They are sitting in their wheelchairs, visiting over lunch at an assisted-living complex. One says, "I am so sorry to have to ask this question because we have been friends for so long, but, Dear, what is your name?" The other looks at her for a long time, then finally replies, "How soon do you need to know?"

Comedians use the fear of Alzheimer's disease or age-related dementia to get laughs, but loss of memory becomes a serious subject as birthdays accumulate. Dr. Kenneth L. Higbee, a professor at BYU and an expert on memory, gives suggestions for staving off memory loss in his book, *Your Memory: How It Works & How to Improve It* (New York: Marlow & Company, 2001).

The first way to preserve memory is to keep learning. According to Dr. Higbee, "You have probably heard the saying that you can't teach an old dog new tricks. Actually, there is another saying that is probably more accurate, but is not quite as well known: 'The quickest way to become an old dog is to quit learning new tricks'" (p. 9). My mother-in-law is a perfect example of someone who has refused to quit learning. Eleven years ago she had a stroke that paralyzed the left side of her body. But that hasn't stopped her from learning to use the computer, writing nearly a hundred poems, and reading every day on a variety of subjects. Many of the aides in her assisted-living home are immigrants from other countries. Every time she meets an aide from a country she hasn't studied, she calls her local librarian, asks for books about that country, and receives them by mail a few days later. I've estimated that she reads more than a thousand pages a week!

Another way to keep memory healthy is to learn and utilize memory-improving techniques. Dr. Higbee writes, "Memory training helps you store information in your brain in such a way that you are more likely to be able to find it and get it out when you want it" (p. 12). He discusses "the Three Rs of Remembering": Recording (acquisition), Retaining (storage), and Retrieving (retrieval). He explains that this "can be illustrated by comparing the memory to a file cabinet. You first type the desired information on a piece of paper (Recording). Then you put it in a file cabinet drawer under the appropriate heading (Retaining). Later you go to the file cabinet, find the information, and get it back out (Retrieving)" (p. 17). Using multiple senses as you record, retain, and retrieve results in even more improvement. If you simply read a fact, you will likely forget it. But if you read and listen to a book on tape, or read a book and then teach the concepts you learned, you are more likely to be able to retrieve the information in the future.

Association, another memory technique, provides one of the best ways to retrieve information. When the First Presidency and the Quorum of the Twelve Apostles issued *The Living Christ* in 2000, the Church museum created an exhibit of art about the Savior to coincide with the document. Because I am a docent at the museum, I have the opportunity of becoming very familiar with its exhibits. I wanted to memorize *The Living Christ.* I did it by thinking of a work of art from the exhibit that illustrated each paragraph, moving in my mind through the exhibit and repeating the paragraph that applied to that work of art. Because the experience was so visual, so audible, and so aesthetic, seven years later I can still quote many of the paragraphs as I recall the visual reminders.

Another way to maintain and improve memory is simply to pay better attention. No matter how much time you spend learning or how knowledgeable you are about memory techniques, it's all for naught unless you first pay attention. Stay focused on the task at hand. If you are wondering if you have broccoli in your teeth as you are being introduced to someone new, you won't remember the person's name. Instead of worrying about your teeth, concentrate on the person and repeat his or her name. Then use the name in the next few sentences of conversation.

Emotional situations can also sidetrack our attention. When I was diagnosed with breast cancer, my oncologist took notes for me during my first appointment with her, which lasted two hours. As she wrote, I was glad she was taking notes, because I knew every medical word would be spelled correctly and I knew the notes would be in perfect outline form. Though I thought it was a nice gesture, however, I didn't fully appreciate it—because I am an audio person and have a good memory for the spoken word. The importance of what Dr. Prystas had done for me was only apparent to me when I got back home and read through her outline. I was shocked at what I hadn't heard.

As you continuously learn, utilize methods to enhance recall, and pay better attention, you will gather greater knowledge about this world. The Lord has promised, "And if a person gains more knowledge and intelligence in this life through his diligence and obedience than another, he will have so much the advantage in the world to come" (D&C 130:19).

Another more personal aspect of memory needs to be mentioned. When you forget, it can tell someone else that he or she is unimportant to you; when you remember, you can build relationships. Karen was visiting another ward. She sat down in Relief Society next to a sister who introduced herself, then asked Karen her name, asked where she was from, and visited with her until the meeting started. Karen felt this sister took special interest in her despite the fact that she was just a visitor. After Relief Society, Sunday school, and sacrament meeting were over, Karen passed this sister on her way to the parking lot. The sister waved and said, "Goodbye, Karen. We'll talk again next time you're here on vacation." When we remember names and facts about a person, we show we care, and the other person feels valued.

It's important to gain and remember knowledge about this world, and it's important to show love and concern by remembering significant facts about others. These, however, are relatively insignificant compared to the covenant of memory we make each week by partaking of the sacrament, when we promise to "*always* remember him" (Moroni 4:3; 5:2; D&C 20:77, 79; emphasis added). We always remember Him when we continuously learn about Him, share testimony of Him, and try to be like Him. When we forget Him, we have spiritual Alzheimer's.

The scriptures help us stave off spiritual forgetfulness. The word *remember* is found approximately 325 times in the scriptures; that's not surprising, since Alma says that the divine purpose of scripture is to enlarge "the memory of this people" (Alma 37:8). Some passages about remembering are divine promises from the Lord, such as, "And their sins and iniquities will I remember no more" (Hebrews 10:17). Some are urgings from prophets, such as, "O remember, remember . . . that there is no other way nor means whereby man can be saved, only through the atoning blood of Jesus Christ . . ." (Helaman 5:9). And others are scriptural memories that help us remember the Lord, His mighty works, and His love for us. He said, "Remember the worth of souls is great in the sight of God" (D&C 18:10).

Memory is a God-given gift. As with all the gifts Heavenly Father bestows on His children, the more we strive to use the gift, the more the gift improves and grows. Let's use techniques to improve our memory, concentrate, focus, and pay attention now so that when we are sitting at lunch with our friend of seventy years, we'll be able to remember her name!

# BUYER'S REMORSE SYNDROME

Buyer's remorse—feelings of anxiety that come after purchasing a big-ticket item, such as a home or automobile—is a common emotional reaction that stems from lack of confidence in one's own judgment. Before you actually make the purchase, all options are open. You have the freedom to choose, and the selection process can be quite exciting. But once you make the choice and sign the contract, all other possibilities cease to be options. When that happens, the previous positive outlook sometimes becomes negative, and you feel stuck.

Buyer's remorse occurs with varying intensity and on a continuum, with extremes on both ends, and it goes without saying that some buyer's remorse is normal. You buy grapes at $1.29 per pound, then see an ad in the newspaper for grapes at $.99 a pound. You buy a blue skirt and two weeks later wish you had purchased the brown one. You order a vegetable platter at a restaurant and when it comes wish you had ordered the quiche.

When buyer's remorse is mild, it is of very little consequence that you paid too much for grapes or that you wish you'd bought a different-colored skirt. But when buyer's remorse swings to the other end of the continuum—causing you to regret what you just ate to the extent that you induce vomiting, or to drop in and out of school repeatedly, or to bounce from job to job or from relationship to relationship—professional counseling may be needed.

A friend once confided that she used to second-guess every decision. Her moment of enlightenment came when she was on her way to return several items she had purchased. She was trying to come up with a reason to give the clerk for why she didn't want the items and why she wanted her money back. The phrase *buyer's remorse* forcefully entered her mind, and she said to herself, "I have buyer's remorse syndrome." Here's how she described what happened next:

"I finally realized that I was being consumed by 'what-might-have-beens.' It was like I was facing forward but walking backward. I was living in the past, rehashing every decision. I was ruining today and my future by worrying about yesterday. This pattern had tremendous power over me before I acknowledged it and started to deal with it.

"As I began to think about my destructive mindset, I came to the conclusion that self-doubt and insecurity are tools of the devil. He was the one telling me I was weak and indecisive and could not trust myself. His message was that the Lord was NOT guiding me—or, worse, that He didn't care."

My friend described finding the following passage in the scriptures: "For the power is in them, wherein they are agents unto themselves" (D&C 58:28). She realized that the Lord had given her *power* to be an *agent*, which meant she had agency and was expected to use it to manage her life. She felt rescued by this concept and wanted to tell everyone she met that she was an agent with power. She said, "Almost immediately after this initial revelation, I felt so much less fear and uncertainty."

Elder Jeffrey R. Holland gave a talk, "Cast Not Away Therefore Your Confidence," which title is a passage from Hebrews 10:35. Elder Holland began his talk by reminding us of the evil that seized Joseph Smith in the grove just before the vision opened to him: "It is the plain and very sobering truth that before great moments, certainly before great spiritual moments, there can come adversity, opposition, and darkness. Life has some of those moments for us, and occasionally they come just as we are approaching an important decision or a significant step in our lives" (Jeffrey R. Holland, "Cast Not Away Therefore Your Confidence," *Ensign,* March 2000, 7).

After reading Elder Holland's talk several times, my friend realized she had cast away her confidence. She wrote, "I had failed to see that the adversary was confusing me (he *is* the author of confusion), and that often opportunity is just around the corner from adversity."

Life teaches by trial and error and through the understanding that there is opposition even in "right" choices. Everyone makes some poor choices. All of us wish we had an eraser to rub out things we regret in the past. But many people with buyer's remorse syndrome doubt themselves throughout their entire lives, and that's not a very fun way to live. It's healthier to take control of the moment, change the present, and by so doing, change the future. With the Lord's help, our confidence and excitement for life will dramatically change. Our spirits will lift, and we will no longer feel powerless and depressed. My friend said, "I am quietly confident and more trusting that the Lord is aware of my needs and will help me make decisions. This provides the confidence I need so that when I do make a 'bad' decision, I view it as a learning opportunity and move on."

As my friend realized, life without excessive buyer's remorse improves. She said, "I can't tell you how much better life is now that I have figured this out. The most amazing thing is when I replaced doubt and fear with faith in my Heavenly Father, I discovered that He had been guiding me all along. I just didn't trust Him enough to see it. My suggestion to all who suffer from buyer's remorse syndrome is admit you have it; identify who the author of doubt and fear is; turn to your Father in Heaven; acknowledge His hand in your life; don't look back with regret, but with thankfulness, and go forward with faith."

# THE IMPORTANCE OF SMALL STUFF

A few years ago I read a small postcard-sized book titled *Don't Sweat the Small Stuff.* It taught the principle that small stuff doesn't matter, and that we should concentrate instead on what is worth "sweating" over. That is useful counsel when used appropriately, but my problem is determining, sometimes in a split second, what is small stuff and what is big stuff—and remembering that what is minutia to me may be enormously important to someone else.

I have another concern with quickly disregarding the small and seemingly insignificant: the voice of the Spirit often communicates as mere nudges and nuances. When a prompting from the still, small voice causes us to act, the concept of "small stuff" being unimportant goes down the drain.

Most of the errands the Holy Ghost prompts us to perform involve kindness, and there is no such thing as a small kindness. Here's a perfect example: One day I was shopping in a sprawling mall when I realized that a very important addressed but unstamped letter had fallen out of my purse. How I worried about that letter! Within a few days, however, I learned that the company the envelope was addressed to had received the letter with the check still inside. What had happened? The only possible explanation is that someone found the letter, stamped it, and mailed it. Is a thirty-nine-cent stamp affixed to someone else's envelope small stuff?

For many years I've had trouble sleeping. I must have already used up all the hormones that help a woman my age get to sleep and stay asleep. I often have to stay in bed ten hours to get five or six hours of sleep; consequently, I am not an early riser. But one morning I woke up early and felt rested, so I got up and began reading and answering my email. As I was doing that, the thought of someone with whom I hadn't communicated for several months crossed my mind. Without thinking it was any kind of prompting, I typed in thirty words, including "Dear" and "Love," and clicked Send. The next morning I was again reading email and noted a reply from my friend that she had written at 10:37 the night before. It read: "Dear Marilynne, when I saw an email from you I was going to write back and ask you if Susan had told you to write me. Then I realized your email was sent at 6:56 this morning. Wow, it's so nice to have a reminder that Heavenly Father cares about me enough to prompt you to write to me TODAY of all days. I was just having a really bad day overall and waiting for ***anything*** to go right today, and your email made me feel loved. Thank you so much." Is a thirty-word email small stuff?

Thinking of how little sleep I get reminded me of a recent Saturday in the Salt Lake Temple, where Richard and I serve as ordinance workers. On Friday night we try to be in bed by 9:00 p.m. because the alarm goes off at 3:30 a.m. to allow us time to get to the temple and change into white by 4:15 for my early prayer meeting. For someone who can't get to sleep or stay asleep on a normal night, this once-a-week ritual is challenging. On this particular night, I had slept fewer than four hours. Somehow I struggled through my assignments for the first hour or two; then I went to the cafeteria, where I ate a bowl of cracked wheat cereal that perked me up enough to carry out the rest of my duties. At 10:50, I changed into my street clothes, and by 11:00 I was sitting in the downstairs lobby waiting for Richard. His responsibilities usually keep him a few minutes longer than mine do.

Sometime after I sat down to wait for him I dozed off. Suddenly, I woke up and looked at my watch. It was 12:17. How could I have possibly slept that long, and where was Richard? I looked around the room and saw him sitting against the opposite wall, where he'd been watching me sleep for almost an hour and a half! How I appreciated that great kindness from the man who always has a million things to do. Is letting a loved one get a much-needed nap small stuff?

A friend told me about the day she had been gardening and realized that in fifteen minutes she had an appointment to meet her visiting teaching companion at the home of a sister they had not yet been able to contact that month. She knew she needed a shower and a change of clothes. She ran to the bathroom, took off her gardening gloves, and turned on the shower when a seven-word thought came: "Don't take a shower; take your gloves." So she turned off the shower and put her gloves in her pocket.

After giving the lesson, her companion had to leave, but my friend lingered behind. My friend still didn't know why she had brought the gloves but decided that if it were a prompting, the sister would know why she had come without showering and with gardening gloves in her pocket. After explaining her appearance, the sister hesitated only a moment before telling her about an outside project she was working on and with which she would very much appreciate help. Is following the promptings of the Spirit small stuff?

No kindness, however small, can be classified as "small stuff." As Professor Higgins says, "It is these little things that matter, Pickering. Take care of the pence and the pounds will take care of themselves is as true of personal habits as of money" (George Bernard Shaw, *Pygmalion,* Act II, line 174, 1916). Alma said it this way: "Now ye may suppose that this is foolishness in me; but behold I say unto you, that by small and simple things are great things brought to pass; and small means in many instances doth confound the wise" (Alma 37:6). Volumes could be written in a series titled, *Do the Small Stuff,* because if we take care of the small stuff, the big stuff takes care of itself.

# FAILURE AVOIDANCE PLANS

Many years ago I attended a two-day seminar taught by a renowned motivational speaker. One of the subjects he taught, failure avoidance, was completely new to me and of such impact that this way of living continues to bless my life today.

The basic concept of failure avoidance is simple: Consider how items on your to-do list might fail; then, one by one, implement plans to insure that potential failures don't happen. Failure avoidance may sound negative, but it's absolutely positive.

Imagine your daughter is performing in her ballet school's concert next Saturday at 7 p.m. in a town twenty miles away. What might cause your daughter to fail in this experience or cause you to fail in being a patient and supportive mother? Factors that might cause failure for your daughter would include being unable to find her ballet slippers or costumes; for you it would include running out of gas, getting lost, or being late.

To help insure success, you make a failure avoidance plan (FAP). You don't get paranoid; you just make your plan and follow through. On Friday, you get gas and have your daughter pack her ballet slippers (both of them), makeup, and pink tights in a small suitcase. You print out driving instructions from the Internet. You plan what you'll eat Saturday afternoon so you can leave fifteen minutes early.

No FAP is foolproof, but your FAP will prevent the most likely setbacks. In the example of the ballet concert, there could be a blizzard or some other thing over which you have no control, but you can be confident that the things you *can* control won't fail.

It might seem that making an FAP is a lot of extra work; it's not. FAPs actually save time, energy, resources, and stress. And as you become more proficient in failure avoidance preparations, your everyday life will become more streamlined. You will accomplish more in a shorter period of time. Best of all, you won't be frantically searching at the last minute for a lost ballet slipper. You won't be frustrated because there is no time to eat, and you won't be contentious when you can't find the place and consequently arrive late.

Failure avoidance respects absolutes such as the laws of nature. Gravity always pulls down; each day has exactly 86,400 seconds; time ticks forward; and calendars never turn back. If you make a perfect soufflé on Saturday but the party you were supposed to take it to was on Friday, you failed. You are wasting sun-block lotion if you're already sunburned. You can't get life insurance coverage on someone who is dead.

Failure avoidance also acknowledges the law of probability. A certain percentage of the time you will be lucky, and everything will work out even if you didn't prepare and implement a failure avoidance plan. Eventually, though, the statistical realities of life will catch up with you.

One night a young mother who needed to go to a warehouse store realized she had fewer than two gallons of gas. Her kind husband usually kept the cars filled, but he had been too busy to take care of it that day. She quickly calculated her van's miles to the gallon and the distance to the store, and decided she could make it. Besides, she hated getting gas—the fumes bothered her, and the children were already tired. Her calculations and excuses almost let her pass the last gas station before the freeway entrance. Then she realized that if she stopped and filled the tank, she wouldn't have to stress about running out of gas. Her FAP was that simple.

She filled the tank, drove to the store, shopped, put the children back in their car seats, loaded the groceries in the van, and turned on the ignition. The gas gauge pointed to full, but she didn't even notice. She had bought full-tank insurance, and she pulled out of the parking lot worry-free.

Within minutes, as she drove up the on-ramp, she became aware that traffic on her side of the freeway was at a standstill, and there were no cars on the other side of the freeway. She spent the next sixty minutes inching along as all vehicles were forced to exit the freeway at the next off-ramp. Now she *was* thinking about the gas tank and was so thankful she had used failure avoidance.

Failure avoidance is actually a part of everyday life that is hardly noticed. You wear a seat belt in the car. You put perishable food in the refrigerator. You go to the dentist, wash your hands, take vitamins, exercise, lock your doors, and carry wipes in your purse. You buy home, health, auto, and life insurance.

We are taught failure avoidance at church—we keep our covenants, read the scriptures, obey the commandments, go to the temple, heed the counsel of the living prophets. We pray and develop testimonies as insurance against spiritual failure. We store water and food and have money available for emergencies. We strive to be debt-free and self-sufficient. In all, we are taught to prepare against a day of need.

The Lord gives the very best reason to practice failure avoidance: "If ye are prepared ye shall not fear" (D&C 38:30). Why didn't the young mother fear running out of gas? Because she had filled up her gas tank—she was prepared.

The opposite of making a failure avoidance plan is taking unnecessary risks. Life has enough inherent risks! We don't need more. Let's protect our spiritual, physical, and emotional lives by making the laws of God, nature, and probability our allies, not our enemies.

# WHAT DOES "ONE ETERNAL ROUND" MEAN TO YOU?

Because of the sacred nature of temple ordinances, members of the Church do not talk about what happens inside the temple. But some things can be talked about. For example, there is an entry about the prayer circle in *The Encyclopedia of Mormonism*:

"The prayer circle is a part of Latter-day Saint temple worship, usually associated with the Endowment ceremony. Participants, an equal number of men and women dressed in temple clothing, surround an altar in a circle formation to participate unitedly in prayer.

"As the ancients came to the altar to communicate and commune with God, so also do members of the Church . . . surround the altar in a prayer circle and in supplication. United in heart and mind, the Saints petition God for his blessings upon mankind, his Church, and those who have special needs.

"The circle is an ancient and universal symbol of perfection. . . . The formation of the prayer circle suggests wholeness and eternity" (Daniel H. Ludlow, ed., *Encyclopedia of Mormonism* [New York: Macmillan Publishing, 1992], 3:1120).

One of my friends once went to the temple hoping to participate in the prayer circle but wondered if too many others had also come with that desire. Usually the officiator asks for a certain number to participate because of space limitations, so she was surprised when the officiator said, "All who want to participate in the prayer circle are welcome." Half the people in the session immediately stood! Perhaps because the circle was so large, the symbolic thought of "one eternal round" came into her mind.

*One eternal round* isn't talked about much. So after hearing the testimony of this sister, I sought a clearer understanding of the concept. Here is what I found.

*One eternal round* is used to describe Heavenly Father's eternal purposes. The Lord God is constant, continuous, and consistent. He is unchanging. " He cannot walk in crooked paths . . . neither hath he a shadow of turning from the right to the left, or from that which is right to that which is wrong . . ." (Alma 7:20). " He is the same from everlasting to everlasting, being the same yesterday, today, and forever . . . without variation" (Joseph Smith, *Lectures on Faith,* 3:15). "The people of the past eternity were saved by the same course of obedience that will bring eternal life to the people of future eternities" (Bruce R. McConkie, *Doctrinal New Testament Commentary,* Vol. 3 [Salt Lake City: Bookcraft, Inc., 1973], 239). God unfolds His mysteries to His children in "times of old as in times to come" (1 Nephi 10:19).

In the King Follett discourse Joseph Smith compares the immortal mind of man to *one eternal round.* "I take my ring from my finger and liken it unto the mind of man—the immortal part, because it has no beginning. Suppose you cut it in two; then it has a beginning and an end; but join it again, and it continues one eternal round. So with the spirit of man" (Joseph Fielding Smith, *Teachings of the Prophet Joseph Smith* [Salt Lake City: Deseret Book Company, 1976], 354).

In his hymn, "If You Could Hie To Kolob," W.W. Phelps used this phrase: "The works of God continue,/ And worlds and lives abound; / Improvement and progression / Have one eternal round" (*Hymns,* 284).

The concept of *one eternal round* is fundamental to faith in God. What if He were a changeable God? What if you couldn't count on Him to tell the truth or if He were arbitrary in granting blessings? What if He might not be available when you needed Him? What if there was the chance that He was having a bad day, or He was sleeping, or on vacation? Doubt would enter your heart. A capricious God would be no better than a golden calf. But because our Father in Heaven is the same yesterday, today, and forever, you can have full confidence in Him.

Does this concept matter to us? Is there a practical application outside the temple? I think there are many. During moments of frustration we can remember Heavenly Father's eternal attributes and His *one eternal round*, and we can try to be more like Him by increasing our patience and consistency with our spouse and children. When we kneel in family prayer, we can reflect on *one eternal round.* As the Primary song says:

> Let us gather in a circle
> And kneel in fam'ly prayer (*Children's Songbook*, 189).

Think of your little family circle increasing forever. Think of inviting your posterity to join you in family prayer a hundred years from now, and consider that a reason to keep searching for ancestors on your family tree. Think of the size of that family circle expanding into eternity—never ending, continuous, and glorious. It is a lovely symbol and thought—whether in your home or in the temple—to ponder Heavenly Father's divine purpose and know that you are part of His *one eternal round.*

# HAPPILY PREPARED EVER AFTER*

As a teen I envisioned my life evolving in fairy-tale fashion. I was confident I would grow up talented and beautiful and that someday my prince would come, sweep me off my feet, and we'd live happily ever after. I now know, as you do, that "happily ever after" doesn't exist in the romantic, Hollywood way I imagined. You noted my immature goals were to be *talented* and *beautiful,* not loving or helpful or honest or virtuous or educated or prepared for whatever life had in store for me. I should have observed that many women are widowed or divorced, that some husbands lose their jobs or become disabled, and that out of necessity there are wives who become the primary breadwinners. I also should have realized that some women never marry.

Mid-way through my senior year of high school, my father sat down with me to give counsel about my future. By using illustrations of women with whom we were acquainted, he let me know that sometimes difficult things happen in life. He told me that I must be prepared to support myself (and any children) as an insurance policy for the future. He asked me where I wanted to go to college. I told him. He said, "No, you will go to the University of Utah." While I was digesting that fact, he asked, "And what do you want to be, a nurse or a teacher? "A nurse," I said. "No," he said, "You should be a teacher."

The conversation was that brief because my father, a school principal, was not a man of many words. But I trusted that he understood my strengths and weaknesses and knew where I would succeed. His concern for my education didn't stop when I fell in love. When

Richard asked my father for my hand in marriage, I still had two quarters before graduation from the University of Utah. My father made Richard promise that my graduation would be his first priority. Richard followed my father's example and extracted the same promise from our sons-in-law.

As events have unfolded, how grateful I am for a father who insisted that I prepare myself for whatever lay before me. I'm grateful I have a degree and a marketable skill, which has enabled me to bring in a little extra income throughout the years and has brought me satisfaction and the ability to serve in ways I otherwise could not have.

If you prepare for a good career and never marry, you still have a fulfilling career. If you prepare for a good career, marry, and never have to be employed a day in your life, you still have a good education—and you have the best insurance policy possible, one that pays dividends. You also have the blessing that comes with being prepared: "ye shall not fear" (D&C 38:30).

Does this counsel apply only to younger women? No. At every stage and age of life we need to plan ahead. If you are not currently working, you may want to prepare for the day when you might need to. If you already have a marketable skill, it may be to your advantage to keep that skill polished and ready to use. You might want to keep current by reading and perhaps taking an occasional class to keep up on the latest in your field.

It is wise to prepare before you actually need to use your skills in the marketplace. Elder L. Tom Perry said in a Worldwide Training Meeting, "We need to maintain good skills to be gainfully employed. In a changing world, we must keep up-to-date, or our skills will become obsolete. Even though we are busy in Church assignments, we should not pass up opportunities to increase our development and improve the welfare of our families. This requires that we invest adequate time and thought to preparing for the future.

"This counsel applies to the sisters as well as the brethren. Although the responsibility to provide for the family belongs primarily to fathers, the proclamation indicates that 'disability, death, or other circumstances' may also require you sisters to use and develop your skills to provide for your families" (L. Tom Perry, "A

Solemn Responsibility to Love and Care for Each Other," *Liahona,* June 2006, 56).

If you do not have a marketable skill you would enjoy using daily, plan now to obtain one. Assess your educational background. List your interests, aptitudes, and talents. Decide how you can obtain a marketable skill with the least amount of money, time, and stress. The important thing is to start. There are a number of educational opportunities, such as four-year college, two-year college, business college, skills centers, vocational schools, community schools, apprenticeship programs, on-the-job training, correspondence or independent study, and continuing education. Prepare for a variety of possible situations: What would you do if it becomes necessary to work full-time? What could you do part-time? What home-based businesses might you consider?

If you are unmarried, are you prepared to spend your entire life in the work force? Don't fall into the trap of seeking entry-level jobs just to fill the time until you get married. Use your time and talent to make a difference in the business world and in your community. If you are a mother and in a situation where you must work, do you find your job satisfying—financially, intellectually, and spiritually? Are there good opportunities for advancement? Do you have a career plan? How can you upgrade your occupational skills? There are agencies in most communities that can help you improve your current skills or help you develop a new career path. Your bishop can also provide counsel and put you in contact with your ward or stake employment specialist.

As you make efforts to improve your career potential, though, remember that "The Family, A Proclamation to the World" instructs us that "Mothers are primarily responsible for the nurture of their children." In your preparations for your future, make the nurture of your children a clear priority over your career.

When Maurine—a thirty-year-old mother of three—was divorced, she could have found a clerical or light-industry job that would have been a source of immediate money. Instead, she returned to the university to complete her nursing degree. Although it took nearly three years, during which time she lived solely on alimony and child support, she is now happily employed at a hospital doing what she loves and enjoying the security of a higher income.

Karen, a thirty-seven-year-old mother of six, found that the demands of a large family were stretching their budget beyond its limits. As the bills began to pile up, she didn't want to leave her children. She and her husband bought some used school equipment and set up a preschool in their basement. Seven years later, her preschool has such an excellent reputation that she has a long waiting list.

Margaret was unable to have children for the first ten years of her marriage. While she waited and hoped for a family, she finished her undergraduate work at a nearby university and then obtained her master's degree. Twelve years and six children later, Margaret was left alone and was fortunately able to secure a teaching job at the university. She feels greatly blessed to have been financially prepared to raise her children alone.

Careful and prayerful preparation at every stage and age will allow us to live rich and fulfilling lives, whatever our "happily ever after" turns out to be.

*Updated from an article, "Happily Prepared Ever After," *Ensign,* July 1985, 65. Used with permission.

# DOES OBEDIENCE MATTER?

A guest speaker arrived at a Relief Society birthday party a few minutes early still a bit confused by the subject on which she had been asked to speak. The Relief Society president had asked her to speak on obedience. "For the Relief Society birthday party?" the speaker asked incredulously. "Yes," the president said. "It's what our sisters need to hear."

In an effort to make the subject interesting, the speaker prepared clue questions with scriptures to spell out O-B-E-D-I-E-N-C-E, kind of like what happens on *Wheel of Fortune.* This is what she came up with:

O— What is the purpose of earth life?

> *"And we will prove them herewith, to see if they will do all things whatsoever the Lord their God shall command them"* (Abraham 3:25).

Answer: To learn obedience.

B— Why did Adam offer sacrifices to the Lord?

> *"And after many days an angel of the Lord appeared unto Adam, saying: Why dost thou offer sacrifices unto the Lord? And Adam said unto him: I know not, save the Lord commanded me"* (Moses 5: 6).

Answer: Because he was obedient.

E—Why are humans less than the dust of the earth?

> *"For behold, the dust of the earth moveth hither and thither . . . at the command of our great and everlasting God"* (Helaman 12:8).

Answer: Because all of God's other creations obey Him implicitly.

D—What happens when we are not humble or obedient in our service?

*"When we undertake to cover our sins, or to gratify our pride . . . the heavens withdraw themselves. . . . Hence many are called, but few are chosen"* (D&C 121:37–40).

Answer: The distinguishing difference between the "called" and the "chosen" is that the "chosen" obey.

I— What is the opposite of stubbornness?

*"And it came to pass that I, Nephi, said unto my father: I will go and do the things which the Lord hath commanded, for I know that the Lord giveth no commandments unto the children of men, save he shall prepare a way for them that they may accomplish the thing which he commandeth them"* (1 Nephi 3:7).

Answer: Obedience.

E—How may all mankind be saved?

*"We believe that through the Atonement of Christ, all mankind may be saved, by obedience to the laws and ordinances of the Gospel"* (Articles of Faith 1:3).

Answer: By obedience.

N—What is the first law of heaven?

*"The first law of heaven is obedience, and every dispensation of truth has required such"* (Jeffrey R. Holland, *Christ and the New Covenant* [Salt Lake City: Deseret Book Company, 1997], 139).

Answer: Obedience.

C—How can you show Heavenly Father and Jesus that you love Them?

*"If ye love me, keep my commandments"* (John 14:15).

Answer: By obeying Them.

E—What do the obedient receive?

*"And they who keep their second estate shall have glory added upon their heads for ever and ever"* (Abraham 3:26).

> Answer: The obedient "who have endured valiantly for the gospel of Jesus Christ" will receive "thrones and dominions, principalities and powers . . ." (D&C 121:29).

When dinner was over, the president introduced the speaker and asked the sisters, who were seated at ten round tables in the cultural hall, to please move the tables to the back and put their chairs in a semi-circle around the lectern. Not one sister moved. She repeated the request, adding that it would be easier on the speaker. One called out, "We'll just turn our chairs around." A few did. The speaker thought this was a strange response to one's Relief Society president, but the president simply shrugged her shoulders and sat down.

The speaker stood and looked at her spread-out audience. She asked the sisters to move so that she wouldn't have to project her voice to the back and corners of the room. A sister called out, "Just deal with it." The speaker thought, "This *is* a ward with an attitude problem. The president was right; they *do* need a lesson in obedience."

When the speaker got home that night, she looked up an *Ensign* article in which she recalled reading about a similar situation:

"I attended a meeting once when the presiding authority invited members of the congregation to come forward in the meeting room. A few stirred. Most did not. Why not?

"I feel sure there were those who questioned why they should leave their comfortable position. 'Why should I?' That question was, no doubt, followed promptly by an excuse or rationalization as to why it should not matter whether the seat was changed or not. I believe there followed some irritation that the presiding authority should make such a request. The last step, obvious to all who observed, was slothfulness in responding. Few moved. Was that a small thing? Yes. But it reflected a deeper, more profound lack of willingness to obey. It reflected a spirit of disobedience. That is not a small thing.

"I was recently in a Church meeting in West Africa when a priesthood leader invited the brethren to come forward and occupy the first three rows of the chapel. Every man immediately stood and moved his seat according to instruction. A small thing? Yes. But it reflected a willingness to obey. That is not a small thing" (H. Ross Workman, "Beware of Murmuring," *Ensign*, November 2001, 85).

A week after speaking to the disobedient Relief Society, the speaker attended her own ward Relief Society birthday party. The same scenario began, but didn't play out. After dinner, when the sisters were asked to move the tables back and the chairs forward, every sister obeyed. Does obedience matter? Yes, on every level.

# DON'T FORFEIT YOUR AGENCY

J. Leo Fairbanks' painting, *The Journey of the Wise Men,* shows three wise men atop loaded camels descending a steep and rocky mountain pass toward the great city of Jerusalem; the glow of the city seems to beckon them. Their faith in the Savior propels them to follow the star divinely positioned to guide true followers of Christ to Him. After arriving in Jerusalem, they discover that King Herod knows nothing of the star or the birth of the Christ child, but that prophecy says Jesus will be born in Bethlehem, not Jerusalem (see Micah 5:2). As they then wend their way toward Bethlehem, they realize that worldly wisdom has caused men to ignore the prophetic signs indicating the Christ child's birth.

The artist wrote an inscription to accompany the painting: "To follow divine direction even the wisest men must surrender their human wisdom to God's will." Elder Neal A. Maxwell expressed this same thought in his final talk, given in the priesthood session of general conference: "As you submit your wills to God, you are giving Him the *only* thing you *can* actually give Him that is really yours to give" ("Remember How Merciful the Lord Hath Been,"*Ensign*, May 2004, 44).

The painting, the inscription, and Elder Maxwell's quote caused me to ponder: Have I surrendered any of my human wisdom—my will—to God? And what exactly is *will,* anyway?

After some study I found that *will* is agency, the ability to choose. The war in heaven, fought between the forces of good and evil, was a confrontation over individual will. The one-third of Heavenly Father's spirit children who followed Satan paid for their choice by forfeiting their chance at mortality. It cost them the opportunity to have a physical body, the prospect of posterity, and a degree of glory after this life. Without agency, there would be no progression.

Since we all earned the opportunity to experience mortality, earth life boils down to the same question: To whom will we surrender our will? The war in heaven still rages on earth. Satan still desires our will and covets and envies our agency. The more we give our will to him, the more he takes from us. As we relinquish our agency to him, one choice at a time, Satan builds a chain to bind us one link at a time. If we surrender our will to him, our eternal progression stops. That's what damnation is. We become slaves to the devil, miserable as he is throughout eternity.

Jesus invites us to give our will to Him when He says, "Come unto me" (Matthew 11:28). If we surrender our will to Him, our opportunities to use our agency broaden—both now and throughout eternity. If we accept His invitation, our progression never stops.

The prophet Lehi clearly stated several facts: "Wherefore, men are free according to the flesh. . . . they are free to choose liberty and eternal life, through the great Mediator of all men, or to choose captivity and death, according to the captivity and power of the devil; for he seeketh that all men might be miserable like unto himself" (2 Nephi 2:27). If this scripture were stated as two equations, it would look like this:

Jesus Christ + your will = liberty
Satan + your will = misery

Lehi provided a similar equation when begging his sons not to "choose eternal death, according to the will of the flesh and the evil which is therein, which giveth the spirit of the devil power to captivate, to bring you down to hell, that he may reign over you in his own kingdom" (2 Nephi 2:29). Here's how that equation looks:

Satan + your will = captivity

Instead, Lehi pleaded with his sons to choose a better way: "I would that ye should look to the great Mediator, and hearken unto his great commandments; and be faithful unto his words, and choose eternal life, according to the will of his Holy Spirit" (2 Nephi 2:28). That way can be illustrated with this equation:

Jesus Christ + your will = eternal life

Let's return to the example of the wise men. A case study in agency and the consequence of choice is provided by the wise men, the chief priests and scribes, and King Herod. The wise men traveled a great distance from the east, which must have taken a long time at significant expense. When they arrived in Jerusalem they boldly stated their purpose and asked, "Where is he that is born King of the Jews? for we have seen his star in the east, and are come to worship him." King Herod asked the chief priests and scribes where Christ was to be born; based on scriptural prophecy, they told Herod and the wise men that the Savior would be born in Bethlehem. Here was the moment of truth: the wise men, the chief priests and scribes, and Herod all had the same information. How did they use their will?

The wise men took righteous action. They hurried to Bethlehem, where they worshiped and presented their gifts to Jesus Christ. The chief priests and scribes took no action. They continued in their routines, knowing but not doing. Herod took damning action. He sent his soldiers to kill all the children in Bethlehem aged two and under.

Life is measured by what we do with our will. God's most precious gift to us is our agency. To follow divine direction, even the wisest of us must surrender that agency to God's will. In a very real way, doing so enables us to go to Bethlehem in worship and bring our gifts to Him who has given us all.

# CHOOSE (OR BE COMPELLED) TO BE HUMBLE

President Ezra Taft Benson said, "God will have a humble people. Either we can choose to be humble or we can be compelled to be humble" ("Beware of Pride," *Ensign,* May 1989, 4). Becoming humble is the lifelong process of yielding one's will to God's will, of doing things His way. Pride, the opposite of humility, is the great sin of Lucifer, who said to the Father, "give me thine honor" (Moses 4:1). Lucifer wanted to be above all men. The antithesis of that is Jesus Christ, who said, "For I came down from heaven, not to do mine own will, but the will of him that sent me" (John 6:38). Jesus came to obey His Father. Lucifer came to dethrone Him.

When we do our own thing—as Frank Sinatra sang in, "I Did It My Way"—we evidence pride, and we are most definitely guilty of that sin. How can I be so sure? Because the scriptures say, "All we like sheep have gone astray; we have turned every one to his own way . . ." (Isaiah 53:6). *All* and *every one* is unmistakably inclusive.

W. W. Phelps—author of fifteen of our current hymns and scribe to Joseph Smith, a man who helped compile the Doctrine and Covenants and who helped write the Prophet's history—was excommunicated for abusing Church funds. In revenge he stirred up opposition, encouraged lawsuits, spread lies and rumors, wrote and published slanderous reports, and fueled the anger of the mobs. His writings gave Governor Boggs ammunition for the extermination order, which resulted in the massacre at Haun's Mill, where nineteen men and boys were slaughtered. Phelps suggested all Mormon property be confiscated, convinced the Saints to give up their weapons, testified against Joseph in court, wrote a condemning affidavit, and betrayed Joseph to the mob. Largely based on his actions and testimony, Joseph Smith and others were imprisoned in Liberty Jail for four months.

From the time he turned against the Prophet, Phelps felt the wrath of God. He and his family were constantly plagued by illness; nothing went right financially, and they became destitute. Phelps believed he was a damned soul who had sinned too deeply to ever be forgiven in this life or the next. He felt he was a Judas.

Joseph Smith knew that Phelps had moved with his family to Dayton, Ohio, and he sent some missionaries to check on their welfare. Finding him contrite, the missionaries suggested he write to the Prophet and beg for forgiveness. On June 29, 1840, in the depths of humility, he wrote: "Brother Joseph. . . . I am as the prodigal son, though I never doubt or disbelieve the fullness of the Gospel. I have been greatly . . . humbled. I have seen the folly of my way. . . . I have done wrong and I am sorry. The beam is in my own eye. . . . I ask forgiveness in the name of Jesus Christ of all the Saints, for I will do right, God helping me. I want your fellowship . . . for our communion used to be sweet. . . . I will make all the satisfaction on every point that Saints of God can require."

I was able to see for myself a similar shift toward humility one Saturday when I was again assigned to be the coordinator in the brides' room in the Salt Lake Temple. I welcomed a bride and her mother. The bride, whom I'll call Katie, was beautiful and looked like a famous fashion model. I gave them brief instructions, and soon mother and daughter began the process of dressing Katie for her marriage. When a couple makes an appointment to be married in the temple, they receive a letter that spells out important instructions. One paragraph to the bride says that all her underclothing must be white. I was involved helping other brides when I heard one of the temple workers standing near Katie say in the kindest voice possible, "You can't wear that." A hush fell over the room. I turned to see that Katie was putting on a full-body, flesh-colored, corset-type undergarment. With every ear in the room attuned to her, the temple worker reminded Katie that her underclothing, as per instruction, had to be white.

Katie protested. The temple worker explained that the temple is not about fashion or doing things your own way, but rather the ways of the temple have been outlined by Deity to teach humility. To merit the privilege of being sealed by His priesthood power in His house, brides should be willing to do so in the Lord's way.

In embarrassment and anger, Katie stomped out of the bride's room to go to her locker. Then remembering that the key to her locker was in the bride's room, she stomped back in, grabbed the key, and stomped back out. I had no idea what to do. Finally, the silence in the room began to subside as brides and temple workers resumed their preparations and I said a quick prayer for wisdom.

I felt prompted to check on Katie. I found her churning with emotion. I could tell that she had put on a white bra. She obviously knew what was expected of her. We looked at each other for what seemed like forever; finally, I uttered an obvious reminder: "It's your wedding day."

"I know," she said, "but I am so frustrated and angry."

I looked at her, again praying for the right words. "We aren't in a hurry," I said. "You can take a few minutes for yourself, and if you'd like, your locker area is large enough for you to kneel in." She wiped some tears away and went in to her locker area. I went back to the bride's room. Before too long, a peaceful and humble Katie returned to the bride's room to finish her preparations.

I know I shouldn't do things "my way," but rather in the Lord's way. I know any beam is in my own eye. Like you, when prideful thoughts enter my mind, I hope I realize it quickly, and that I have the trust to figuratively kneel in my locker.

# SUNDAY VACATIONS

My patriarchal blessing warns me about participating in activities that are not in harmony with the commandment to keep the Sabbath day holy. It specifically instructs me to avoid places of amusement on the Sabbath, to attend my meetings, and to partake of the sacrament worthily. Consequently, I've always felt extra incentive to be in church every week. When I'm at home, this is not a problem, but when I'm vacationing away from home, observing the Sabbath properly has sometimes been a challenge.

A few years ago I found myself alone in a hotel in San Francisco on the Sabbath. I had done my research before leaving home, and I knew the closest ward was the Bay Ward. Their meetings began at 11:00, and I had figured out how to get a taxi both ways. After checking in at the hotel, I double-checked the information I had gotten on the Internet. I called the number listed on the meetinghouse locator, and the recording verified the information I already had. At about 9:30 Sunday morning, I decided to call once more before I finished getting ready and called for a taxi. The message had changed: "On Sunday, August 18, the Bay Ward will not be holding meetings in the Bay Ward chapel. We invite you to worship with us at stake conference in San Mateo from nine to eleven o'clock."

I just hate it when a plan doesn't work. It was impossible to get to San Mateo before the meeting ended. I wanted to go to church, and felt frustrated that I wouldn't receive my spiritual nourishment for the week. Thinking through my options, I decided to have my own worship service.

I finished getting dressed in my Sunday clothes, looked through the conference edition of the *Ensign* that I had brought with me, and chose two articles to use as talks. (I felt as though I were literally inviting two Apostles to speak.) Then I took a deep breath and welcomed myself to "church." I sang my favorite hymn, said the opening prayer, and read aloud the two talks from the *Ensign*. (It was like having the Apostles there, because as I read I could hear their voices.) I sang the closing hymn and said the closing prayer.

I know private worship services are not part of the Lord's regular plan, but this was an emergency, and I felt blessed by the experience and spiritually ready for the week ahead. Of course, there was no way to compensate for the true purpose of sacrament meeting—partaking of the sacrament.

Earlier this year, Richard and I drove to Telluride, Colorado, on a Saturday. Since we had been up since 3:30 a.m. to fulfill our duties in the temple, had left the temple about noon, and had already been on the road for almost eight hours, we were very tired. I was driving to give Richard a rest. It was getting dark, and I hoped we were almost there. Then I saw a road sign: "Telluride—57 miles." We were still an hour from Telluride. I was not only tired of being on the road, but I was physically and mentally fatigued because I had been up for more than eighteen hours.

As I drove up the mountain, I thought of the approaching Sabbath. I had done the research and knew the closest ward was in Montrose, Colorado, ninety minutes from Telluride. I knew the meetings started at 11:00. The prospect of arriving in Telluride at 9:30 p.m. only to be up, showered, dressed, and on the road again by 9:15 the next morning seemed impossible to me at that moment.

What happened next was scary: I remembered my solitary Sunday in San Francisco. "What a great idea," I mused. I thought how wonderful it would be to have a private worship service with Richard. I even thought of a subject I could teach him and wondered what he would teach me. Just as I was going to suggest my plan to Richard, a still, small voice whispered, "You are being tempted."

I paused, pondered the subtlety of the temptation, and realized what I had to do. I said nothing to Richard about my alternative plan. I got up the next morning, drove the hour and a half, worshipped with the Montrose Colorado First Ward, and spent the rest of the day in silent prayers of gratitude for the tender mercies that were awaiting us as we partook of the sacrament and of the Spirit with the Saints in Montrose. It was as though the entire block of meetings had been planned specifically for us.

The blessings of obeying the commandment to "Remember the sabbath day, to keep it holy" (Exodus 20:8) far outweigh any rationalized inconvenience. Emergency circumstances may arise that may make attending Sunday meetings impossible—as when I was in San Francisco—but the Telluride situation was not that kind of exception. This was my opportunity to show my love for the Lord, who doesn't ask His children to do anything He doesn't do. He keeps the Sabbath day holy: "And on the seventh day God . . . rested . . . from all his work which he had made" (Genesis 2:2). I think that's a significant fact. Keeping the Sabbath day holy is a way to be like God, which should be more than sufficient motivation to get up Sunday morning and get to church, where we will be taught by the Spirit, cleansed by worthily partaking of the sacrament, and blessed in our temporal needs.

The temporal blessings of righteous Sabbath observance are very specific:

> "The fulness of the earth is yours, the beasts of the field and the fowls of the air, and that which climbeth upon the trees and walketh upon the earth;
>
> "Yea, and the herb, and the good things which come of the earth, whether for food or for raiment, or for houses, or for barns, or for orchards, or for gardens, or for vineyards;
>
> "Yea, all things which come of the earth . . ." (D&C 59:16–18).

Some of my best vacation memories are of attending church. The surroundings and languages may be unfamiliar, but the essentials are all there—the same priesthood and sacrament prayers; the same prophets, Apostles, scriptures, and hymns; the same Primary, Relief Society, Young Men, and Young Women; and the same warmth and friendliness. Wherever we meet with the Saints, whether in our home ward or in another country, the Church and the Spirit are the same. And in addition to enhancing our vacation experience by attending church, we receive spiritual and temporal blessings for keeping the Sabbath day holy. You can't beat that!

# THE LATEST ASSAULT ON THE HOLY GHOST

More than twenty million people own iPods, those tiny miracles of technology that allow us to privately listen to an infinite number of musical selections twenty-four hours a day, seven days a week. The improved digital sound quality allows every instrument and voice to be heard with amazing clarity, transforming the head into a concert hall, Broadway theater, rock concert, bar, lounge, or even a gutter. You don't have to worry about getting the best seat in the house, because it's reserved for you—and the only music played is the music *you* want to hear.

Now consider this: approximately twenty million people have hearing loss—and two-thirds of them are under the age of sixty-five. As wonderful as music can be, music listening habits are a primary cause of hearing loss. Hearing loss occurs when loud noises bombard the ear over time. The louder the noise, the less time it takes to cause permanent hearing loss. In today's culture, loud and good seem synonymous, and you probably won't disturb the neighbor next door even if your iPod is at maximum volume.

As you know, noise levels are measured in decibels (dB). A normal conversation is 60 dB. Restaurant noise is ranked at 70 dB, a busy street could be 90 dB, a factory is about 100 dB, and dance clubs are usually 110 dB. A car stereo is 120 dB, a rock concert is 130 dB, a gunshot is 140 dB, and a jet taking off is 150 dB. Hearing damage will occur after 4 hours at 95 dB, after 2 hours at 100 dB, after 30 minutes at 110 dB, and after only 7.5 minutes at 120 dB.

"Noise-induced hearing loss affects both the quantity and the quality of sound. Understanding human speech becomes difficult because words become indistinct. Excessive sound exposure damages hearing by over-stimulating the tiny hair cells within the inner ear. There are between 15,000 and 20,000 of these microscopic sensory receptors in the cochlea (coke-lee-ah). When these hair cells are damaged, they no longer transmit sound to the brain. Sounds are muffled. Hearing damage through noise exposure is permanently lost. Hearing aids amplify the remainder of your hearing. (That deserves restating, hearing aids only amplify what is left of your hearing.)

Is your hearing at risk? These are the warning signs:

"After exposure to loud music or noise you may experience one or more of the following:

- Ringing or buzzing in the ears
- Slight muffling of sounds
- Difficulty in understanding speech. You can hear all the words, but you can't understand them
- Difficulty in hearing conversation in groups of people when there is background noise, or in rooms with poor acoustics" (www.hearnet.com).

The loss of physical hearing isn't the only troubling effect. I've been concerned for years that loud music blocked potential promptings from the Holy Ghost. There were times my children couldn't even hear *me,* and my voice isn't nearly as still and small as that of the Holy Ghost. I've called to a teenager in his room who was mesmerized by loud music and found he couldn't hear me. He didn't even hear a knock on the door. I watched one day as the driver of a car, listening to loud music, failed to yield to a police car with sirens wailing. But these experiences are minor compared to ignoring or being unable to hear the Spirit.

The Doctrine and Covenants begins with the word "hearken"—which means "listen." Nephi tells us, "Therefore I did obey the voice of the Spirit . . ." (1 Nephi 4:18). What would have happened if Nephi had iPod earphones in his ears and hadn't obeyed the voice of the Spirit?

Here's another: "Behold they were manifest unto the prophet by the voice of the Spirit; for by the Spirit are all things made known unto the prophets" (1 Nephi 22:2). And it's not just the prophets: ordinary people can also hear the voice of the Spirit. "And the Spirit giveth light to every man that cometh into the world; and the Spirit enlighteneth every man through the world, that hearkeneth to the voice of the Spirit" (D&C 84:46).

The Lord told Oliver Cowdery, "Yea, behold, I will tell you in your mind and in your heart, by the Holy Ghost, which shall come upon you and which shall dwell in your heart.

"Now, behold, this is the spirit of revelation; behold, this is the spirit by which Moses brought the children of Israel through the Red Sea on dry ground.

"Therefore this is thy gift; apply unto it, and blessed art thou, for it shall deliver you out of the hands of your enemies, when, if it were not so, they would slay you and bring your soul to destruction.

"Oh, remember these words, and keep my commandments. Remember, this is your gift" (D&C 8:2–5).

This is your gift as a confirmed member of the Church of Jesus Christ of Latter-day Saints. So watch out for spiritual iPods and high-decibel activities. Protect your hearing so you can hear the sounds of nature, the voices of those you love, and the precious voice of the Holy Ghost.

# SUCKED IN BY A WORLDLY PHILOSOPHY

Have you ever assumed something was true, made decisions about your life based on that "truth," and later realized you'd been sucked in by a worldly philosophy? I imagine everyone has, because the world is so full of false philosophies. How can you know which, if any, of the ideas glibly tossed around by politicians, Hollywood's rich and famous, and radio and television talk show hosts are true?

Man-made philosophies may sound reasonable, even appealing, but they all lead to the decay of individuals and ultimately of entire civilizations. History has repeatedly shown that after a few generations believe such "truths," societies find themselves wandering in forbidden paths toward complete destruction. Think of the Jaredites, the Greeks, the Romans, and the Nephites. The decline and fall of these great civilizations began as false philosophies ensnared one person at a time. Will Americans be added to the list of great civilizations that have fallen?

The Apostle Paul advised the Colossians: "Beware lest any man spoil you through philosophy and vain deceit, after the tradition of men, after the rudiments of the world, and not after Christ" (Colossians 2:8). *Spoil you* is a frightening phrase. What causes spoilage? How does a person rot? According to Paul, people rot when they are deceived by worldly philosophies—which are the traditions of men—and fail to follow Christ. The Lord warned: "For there are many yet on the earth among all sects, parties, and denominations, who are blinded by the subtle craftiness of men, whereby they lie in wait to deceive . . ." (D&C 123:12).

Let's analyze one such "truth." M. Scott Peck began the first chapter of his book, *The Road Less Traveled* (New York: Simon and

Schuster, Touchstone Books, 1978), with a three-word sentence: "Life is difficult." There is plenty of evidence that accident, disease, disappointment, loss, injury, pain, death, and the consequences of sin and evil are *difficult.* Dr. Peck continues, "This is a great truth, one of the greatest truths." As you read these words, you notice the word *truths* is followed by an asterisk. Your eyes jump to the bottom of the page and read what follows the asterisk: "The first of the 'Four Noble Truths' which Buddha taught was 'Life is suffering.'"

Would any thinking person debate "life is difficult" with Dr. Peck? Would you challenge Buddha's premise that "life is suffering"? British philosopher Bertrand Russell (1872–1970) saw life even more grimly. He equated life with "unyielding despair" (*A Free Man's Worship*, first published in 1903). Is life *difficult, suffering,* or *filled with unyielding despair?* Where can the answer be found?

The answer about the true nature of life is found in the words of the prophets. The prophet Lehi spoke the truth when he said: "For it must needs be, that there is an opposition in all things" (2 Nephi 2:11). Read that again, emphasizing the word *opposition.* That's what is true. Life is comprised of opposing forces! To say that life is *difficult* or *suffering* or filled with *unyielding despair* is as erroneous as saying life is easy, carefree, or filled with continual bliss. Peck, Buddha, and Russell told a half-truth. And many believed it to be the whole truth.

From the beginning of human history, the Lord taught Adam and Eve that life is full of opposites. They learned contrast by experiencing life first in the Garden of Eden and then in the world. They learned the difference between being naked and clothed and being in God's presence and cast out of His presence. They learned for themselves both the benefits and consequences of using agency.

In the Book of Mormon we learn of a civilization that lived "after the manner of happiness" for almost two hundred years. During the next two hundred years they annihilated themselves by believing and acting on false philosophies that resulted in ever-increasing depravity. "The foolish build upon the shifting sands of ethics and the marshlands of manmade philosophies and doctrines" (Robert Millet, *Steadfast and Immovable: Striving for Spiritual Maturity* [Salt Lake City: Deseret Book Company, 1992], 140).

Through your own experiences, you learn the difference between selfish and unselfish, impatience and long-suffering, contention and peace; and like me, you like yourself better when you are unselfish, long-suffering, and at peace. You've learned that happiness isn't found in seeking personal pleasure but in seeking the happiness of others.

There is more to this concept. The patriarch Abraham taught that happiness comes in degrees when he used the phrase "greater happiness" (Abraham 1:2). What is *greater* happiness? It is having the kind of life the Lord Jesus Christ gives. "I am come that they might have life, and that they might have *it* more abundantly" (John 10:10). What is more abundant happiness? It is joy. As Lehi told his son, "men are that they might have joy" (2 Nephi 2:25). Happiness lasts longer than pleasure, and joy lasts longer than happiness. Joy comes progressively as eternal truths are understood and lived.

Does it matter, then, if you think life is difficult? Yes, because it is a half-truth, and by acting on a false foundation we build on shifting sands. When you realize that life is not difficult but is made up of opposing forces, the precious gift of agency becomes even more crucial. Your choices move you toward an eternity with "God and his Christ" (D&C 105:32) or away from Them into the darkness.

Let's watch out for false philosophies that pervert the Lord's "great and eternal plan" of happiness (Alma 34:16). Let's question worldly assumptions and pray for discerning wisdom that we won't get sucked in by the philosophies of men.

# DON'T WALK OR RUN—GALLOP

Recently I had the opportunity to be in rural Idaho with nothing to do except bind a quilt and look out over several farms for a couple of hours. As I sewed, I watched farmers with high-tech machines working the almost-ready-to-harvest hay and potatoes. I listened to the birds singing their mid-day melodies, and watched them swooping and soaring on the breeze. In the field closest to me, three powerful-looking horses munched a little grass here and there but mostly just stood, seemingly enjoying the reverie with me. Then I heard a whistle—the kind of whistle you make with a couple of fingers in your mouth. In response, the horses galloped toward their master.

I immediately thought of my bishop, who had just called me to be the Primary pianist. This made four callings for me. The bishop apologized for calling me to another position, but said that no matter who else he tried to think of, he felt strongly that I was the one for that position. His exact words were, "I don't know how long you will serve in this calling, but I do know for right now you belong in Primary."

Honestly, I didn't want to be in Primary. I had served almost eleven continuous years in Primary a few years earlier. I love children. I love Primary. I have a testimony of Primary. I know the Spirit attends Primary, but I wanted to go to Sunday school to hear Richard's gospel doctrine lessons. And one more responsibility was one more stress, even if little preparation was required. I continued to feel over-burdened until I was set apart. The bishop's counselor blessed me with the ability to get everything done and let me know that this call was from the Lord. I realized that I hadn't exactly galloped toward my Master.

Elder Neal A. Maxwell wrote, "If you had asked me, 'Can a person accept too many callings in a branch or a ward and get too overloaded in terms of the time left for family, work, community, and so forth,' the answer would be yes, in the sense that you ask. But if we ask ourselves, 'Am I doing quite enough to help further the Lord's work,' then our answer must be no. Most of us can do a better job of managing our time and our talents than we do, but it is important to do as the Lord suggested—to run no faster than we are able. . . .

"I am personally persuaded, however, that there are no idle moments, only idle people. I have yet to meet the perfect manager of time. I am not talking about the mere ritual of doing things, but of our using our free agency in such a way that we do the things that matter most, so that these things are not at the mercy of the things that matter least. The Lord will help us before we have reached such limits as we may have" (Neal A. Maxwell, *Deposition of a Disciple* [Salt Lake City: Deseret Book Company, 1976], 58). Elder Maxwell didn't even let leukemia stand in the way of his calling.

My sister Sheila was called to be the stake Primary president. A few weeks later, she and her husband were summoned to the stake president's office and called as a couple to be in charge of the following year's stake youth conference. Sheila is in a very busy stage of life and was shocked at the second call. In her nice way, she reminded the stake president of her other calling. He said, "Oh, don't worry about that. Just accept the call and let's get you set apart."

In her setting-apart blessing, she was promised that time would be compressed, allowing her to accomplish more in less time and that she would have energy for her family and for her calling. The youth conference call increased her testimony of various ways work can be accelerated, how others are raised up to help, and how literally Heavenly Father blesses His servants. During the weeks before the youth conference, she called me several times to share specifics as her blessing was fulfilled, for she not only accomplished all her routine duties, but she also completed extra jobs and her house stayed as clean as ever. In addition, she had the incredible blessing of working closely with her husband, overseeing a successful youth conference, making new friends in the stake, and watching the hand of the Lord hover over her family.

A person really calls him or herself to a calling by accepting or rejecting. This is how it works: The bishop needs to fill a position in the ward. He prays for guidance. He receives inspiration. He calls the person to the calling. If the person thinks it comes from the Lord, he or she accepts and thus allows him or herself to be called. If the person thinks the calling comes from the bishop, he or she may reject the call, denying him or herself the calling and the accompanying blessings.

Six principles emerge and merge:

**Show your faith.** Some may believe that you cannot serve God while serving your family or vice versa. That is not true. God does not compete against Himself. He has more interest in your family than you do.

**Build the kingdom of God.** Brigham Young said, "To me it is the Kingdom of God or nothing upon the earth" (*Discourses of Brigham Young,* selected and arranged by John A. Widtsoe [Salt Lake City: Deseret Book Company, 1954], 444). John Taylor said, "We say it is the kingdom of God or nothing" (*Journal of Discourses,* 6:18)! And Joseph F. Smith said, "'I am for the kingdom of God, or nothing.' Zion, first and foremost. Seek first the kingdom of God and His righteousness, that all other things may be added in the due time of the Lord, and in accordance with His pleasure" (*Conference Report,* April 1909, 3–4).

**Support your family.** When Elder Boyd K. Packer was a young Apostle, he received a request to speak in Denver on Christmas Eve. President Harold B. Lee saw the letter and said, "Don't bother to answer it. I will." President Lee wrote: "Elder Packer will not be able to come on Christmas Eve. He has a previous appointment with his own family" (Lucile C. Tate, *Boyd K. Packer: A Watchman on the Tower* [Salt Lake City: Bookcraft, Inc., 1995], 136).

**Be diligent.** "And see that all these things are done in wisdom and order; for it is not requisite that a man should run faster than he has strength. And again, it is expedient that he should be diligent, that thereby he might win the prize; therefore, all things must be done in order" (Mosiah 4:27). "Be diligent unto the end" (D&C 10:4).

**Be anxiously engaged.** The Lord said, "Be anxiously engaged in a good cause, and do many things of [your] own free will, and bring to pass much righteousness"(D&C 58:27).

**Sacrifice.** The Prophet Joseph Smith said, "Let us here observe, that a religion that does not require the sacrifice of all things never has power sufficient to produce the faith necessary unto life and salvation . . ." (*Lectures on Faith* [Salt Lake City: Deseret Book Company, 1985], 6:7).

When the Master whistles, let's not hesitate. Let's go to Him at a full gallop!

# LET'S WALK AND TALK ABOUT THE SCRIPTURES

Several friends and I go walking on weekday mornings. Our friendships are close, the walking is aerobic, and the fresh air is invigorating. We walk at a quick pace, but never too fast to talk—because more important than boosting our heart rates is lifting one another's spirits. Our conversations center on gospel topics as they relate to situations affecting our lives at the moment. Quite often the topic of the day will pivot around something one of us has read in the scriptures. I treasure these times and come home ready for the day.

We know that the scriptures can be a great source of help. My daughter-in-law Shonna dreamed she and some family members were in a dense jungle. They knew their lives were in jeopardy, and they were very frightened. Suddenly a man with dark eyes stepped out of the trees wearing Book of Mormon-era clothing. He stretched out his arm, took Shonna by the hand, and said, "Do not be afraid; I will help you. My name is Alma."

Alma, or any other person in the scriptures, can't help us unless we release them from their confinement between the covers of our scriptures. If we don't read and reflect on their words, it is as though they didn't exist. I hope you have followed Nephi's counsel to "feast upon the words of Christ" (2 Nephi 32:3). I hope you've found in them "the words of Christ [that] will tell you all things what ye should do" (2 Nephi 32:3). I hope you think of the scriptures as an opportunity to hear God's voice.

One of my favorite experiences reading one of the standard works from cover to cover came in August 2005 when President Gordon B. Hinckley challenged members and friends of the Church to read the

Book of Mormon before the end of the year. My husband let me read all 531 pages aloud to him. I have never learned or felt more as I both saw and heard those sacred words. Reading aloud more than doubles the experience for me. And reading straight through, of course, is only one of many ways to enjoy and learn the scriptures.

Recently I watched Dr. Robert J. Matthews explain how the italicized words came to be in the King James Version of the Bible. Will you be my walking partner today and let me share my new knowledge with you?

Dr. Matthews was doing a BYU Television special on the Joseph Smith Translation of the Bible (JST). To illustrate some of Joseph Smith's changes, he explained that the italicized words in the King James Version of the Bible are there because Hebrew and Greek don't always line up perfectly with English in the translation process. When the King James scholars came to words or phrases that would not translate directly, they made educated guesses and added a word or two in order to make the meaning clear in English. These additions were printed in italics to let readers know that they were not in the original text. Throughout his inspired amending process, Joseph Smith corrected some of these italicized words and phrases.

Brother Matthews gave two examples. In Luke 8:23, Jesus is asleep in the ship during a severe storm. The verse reads: "But as they sailed he fell asleep: and there came down a storm of wind on the lake; and they were filled *with water,* and were in jeopardy." Look at the italics. Who or what was filled *with water?* There was only one boat; so it can't be the boat or "they" would be "it." Perhaps "they" refers to the Apostles. If so, how are Apostles "filled with water"? Brother Matthews directed his audience to look at footnote 23a, which reads: "JST [meaning from the Joseph Smith Translation] Luke 8:23 . . . and they were filled with *fear,* and were in *danger.*" Neither the ship nor the Apostles were filled with water. The Apostles were filled with fear!

Next he cited John 2:24, in which Jesus is celebrating Passover and performing miracles in Jerusalem. The verse reads: "But Jesus did not commit himself unto them, because he knew all *men.*" What does "knew all *men*" mean? In the context it seems confusing. Brother Matthews referred to footnote 24c, which reads: "JST John 2:24 . . .

all *things.*" Jesus Christ knows "all things." Oh, that's so much clearer!

I'm grateful for the integrity of the King James scholars. But I'm also very thankful for the Prophet Joseph Smith, a farm boy who had very little formal schooling. When responding to a question about the authorship of the Book of Mormon, Joseph's wife Emma said that before the Lord began tutoring Joseph "he could neither write nor dictate a coherent and well-worded letter" (Dean C. Jessee, "New Documents and Mormon Beginnings." *BYU Studies,* Vol. 24, No. 4, 1984). And yet, with the Lord's help, he was able to correct the King James scholars!

I watched one of the roundtable discussions about the Book of Mormon on BYU Television. In passing, one of the professors mentioned that the word *plan* did not appear in the Bible. Using my computerized scripture program, I checked. Sure enough, the word *plan* is not in the Bible. This was exciting to me, because I remember the Lord telling Nephi that "many plain and precious things [have been] taken away from the book . . . of the Lamb of God [the Bible]" (1 Nephi 13:28), and this is a crucial example.

I subsequently checked the Book of Mormon and found that the purpose and scope of Heavenly Father's plan is taught multiple times and that *the plan* has five different names—the plan of happiness, redemption, mercy, salvation, and deliverance. As I searched more, I discovered that *great* came before *plan* in some of the references: the *great* plan of *redemption* (Jacob 6:8), the *great* plan of *mercy* (Alma 42:31), the *great* plan of *salvation* (Alma 42:5), the *great* plan of *happiness* (Alma 42:8). I also found that in two places, *eternal* also describes the plan, "the great and eternal plan of redemption" (Alma 34:16) and "the great and eternal plan of deliverance" (2 Nephi 11:5). After reading all these scriptures and feeling the accompanying spirit, I felt Nephi's joy when he exclaimed: "O how *great* the *plan* of our *God!"* (2 Nephi 9:13, emphasis added).

Every time I have experiences like these in the scriptures, I feel like singing the Primary song "Search, Ponder, and Pray," with words by Jaclyn Thomas Milne:

> I love to read the holy scriptures,
> And, ev'ry time I do,

I feel the Spirit start to grow within my heart—
A testimony that they're true. . .
(*Children's Songbook,* 109).

Let's walk and talk again soon!

# IS YOUR RELIGION VAIN?

The tongue has both destructive and elevating power. James, the brother of the Savior, warned, "If any [wo]man among you seem to be religious, and bridleth not [her] tongue, but deceiveth [her] own heart, this [wo]man's religion is vain" (James 1:26). James gives us only two options: either we bridle our tongue, or our religion is vain. What kind of message does our tongue tell about us and the church to which we belong?

A stressed-out woman on a busy boulevard was tailgating the man in front of her. Suddenly the light turned yellow just in front of him. He did the right thing and stopped at the crosswalk, even though he could have gunned it and accelerated through the intersection. The tailgating woman hit the roof, leaned on the horn, and screamed in frustration as she missed her chance to get through the intersection behind him.

As she was still in mid-rant, she heard a loud tap on her window, and she looked up at a police officer with a very serious expression on his face. The officer ordered her to get out of the car with her hands up. He handcuffed her and took her to the police station, where she was searched, fingerprinted, photographed, and placed in a cell.

A few hours later a policeman approached the cell and opened the door. The woman was escorted back to the booking desk where the arresting officer was waiting with her personal effects. He said, "I'm very sorry for this mistake. You see, I pulled up behind your car while you were blowing your horn and cussing a blue streak. I noticed the 'Choose the Right' license plate holder, the 'Go Cougars' and 'Come with me to Primary' bumper stickers, and the chrome-plated 'What

Would Jesus Do?' emblem on the trunk. Naturally I assumed you had stolen the car."

Whether you and I like it or not, membership in The Church of Jesus Christ of Latter-day Saints makes us walking and talking representatives of Jesus Christ. How I conduct myself outside the meetinghouse makes a difference. As illustrated by the fictitious story of the stressed-out woman driver, in a moment of frustration or anger we can harm the reputation of the Church or its members.

As a church, we send more than 53,000 missionaries into the world at a cost that exceeds $20 million a month. We pray for the missionaries and sign up to feed them dinners. As mothers we prepare our sons and daughters to serve missions. So why would we sabotage their efforts to "bring the world His truth"? In James's language, if my tongue is not in sync with my professed beliefs, my "religion is vain." Actually, it's worse than vain—because getting angry and "cussing a blue streak" with Church mottos on the car is doing "anti-missionary" work. As Alma said to his son Corianton, "when [the people] saw your conduct they would not believe in my words" (Alma 39:11).

Carolyn, a clerk in a busy candy store, was working alone one afternoon because the other employee had gone home sick. The store's layout made it difficult for employees to serve customers in the order in which they came in to the store. Carolyn was trying to be vigilant, but as she started to help one customer, another customer began yelling. The angry woman's comments included statements about Carolyn's intelligence. The woman concluded with a threat to report Carolyn to the manager. Carolyn wisely got to the manager before the woman did. The manager responded, "Oh, that's just Mrs. Jones; she comes in here a lot. Don't fret over her. I know what kind of an employee you are."

Carolyn thought she had put the incident behind her until she moved into a new ward a few months later; the angry customer was a member of her new ward. Neither Carolyn nor the sister ever spoke of the incident, but Carolyn knew the woman remembered because of the many kindnesses she did for Carolyn and her family. Carolyn felt she was trying to make up for her outburst months earlier at the candy store.

You have your frustrating moments, as do I. Most all of us sometimes say or do things we wish we hadn't and are guilty of what could be called "anti-sisterly" conduct, as in what happened at the candy store. The fact is that wherever we are and whatever we do, others observe our words and actions and make judgments about either the Church or about the strength of our religious convictions. My words and actions affect you; your words and actions affect me; and we affect everyone with whom we come in contact.

Whenever I find myself in an exasperating situation, I try singing in my mind the hymn, "As Sisters in Zion." The words of the second verse help me through any temptation to be anti-missionary and/or anti-sisterly:

> The errand of angels is given to women;
> And this is a gift that, as sisters, we claim:
> To do whatsoever is gentle and human,
> To cheer and to bless in humanity's name
> (*Hymns,* 309)

These elevating words by Emily H. Woodmansee are a mission statement for the women of the Church. One day as I sang this verse, I thought of a one-word change that would make the message even stronger but that would spoil the rhyming pattern. (Sister Woodmansee likely thought of it herself, but elected to stay with the word that rhymed.) If "human" didn't have to rhyme with "woman," I'd change "human" to "Christlike," which would raise a woman's sights higher and explain the loftiest reason why women serve.

The next time I feel annoyed or impatient, I'll remember that my actions and words are an advertisement for or against Jesus Christ and His Church. I hope I'll remember that I am a sister in Zion. When I see a need, I hope I'll respond both in humanity's and Christ's name. But as you know, *hope* is not good enough. *Hope* is not an action. I must "*do* whatsoever is gentle" and Christlike, and "*cheer* and . . . *bless* in humanity's name." Then my religion will not be vain.

# REACHING OUT TO THE PRIESTHOOD

I can make banana bread, but I can't make a banana—nor can I make flour, sugar, salt, butter, eggs, or pecans. I can hike a mountain, but I can't organize the elements into a wildflower, a rock, or even a weed, let alone a magnificent mountain with its singular silhouette. I can balance my checkbook (most of the time) but I can't do equations that hold stars and planets in their orbits. I can give comfort to my dying father, but I cannot separate his spirit from his body, transport him to his next sphere, or reunite his body and spirit in a glorious resurrection. But the priesthood of God can.

The priesthood *is God's power*. During the April 2005 priesthood session of general conference, Elder Jeffrey R. Holland explained that Charles Wesley criticized his brother John, one of the founders of the Methodist Church, for ordaining a Mr. Coke to the priesthood without God's authority. Charles wrote:

> How easily are bishops made
> By man or woman's whim;
> Wesley his hands on Coke hath laid,
> But who laid hands on him?
> ("Our Most Distinguishing Feature," *Ensign,* May 2005, 43)

Beginning with Adam, priesthood lines of authority were recorded in the Bible. Today, every man who holds the priesthood in the Church of Jesus Christ of Latter-day Saints can trace his authority to Joseph Smith and then to Jesus Christ. We know who laid hands on whom. *Receiving* the priesthood, however, is conditional upon worthiness. I have seen righteous men who use their priesthood as "the power of God unto salvation" (Romans 1:16) increase in spirituality. I have also seen men who use their priesthood casually stagnate or decrease in spirituality.

The priesthood is *God's* power to bestow on whomever He chooses, and its exercise is conditional on worthiness. Early in his life, King Saul became involved in a war that was not going well. He sent for the prophet Samuel, asking that Samuel make sacrifices so the Lord would reveal how to win the war. Saul waited and waited, but Samuel didn't arrive before Saul's patience expired. Saul then made a grave mistake: although he was not a priest, he decided he could offer sacrifice as well as could the prophet.

When Samuel arrived and discovered what Saul had done, he said: "Thou hast done foolishly" (1 Samuel 13:13). Saul's presumptuous attempt to use priesthood he didn't have caused the Lord to prophesy through Samuel, "thy kingdom shall not continue" (1 Samuel 13:14).

The Israelites were commanded to "make . . . fringes in the borders of [your] garments . . . that ye may look upon [them], and remember all the commandments of the LORD . . ." (Numbers 15:38–39). Jesus wore this fringe. The woman with a twelve-year issue of blood reached out and touched this fringe and was healed. Her faith gave her the courage to reach out to the priesthood. Unknowingly, the lame man who asked for money each day at the temple gates also reached out to the priesthood. When he reached up to Peter and John, expecting a few coins, the Apostle Peter said, "Silver and gold have I none; but such as I have give I thee: In the name of Jesus Christ of Nazareth rise up and walk" (Acts 3:6). Men, women, and children can reach out to the priesthood and be healed. The priesthood is God's power to heal.

The Apostles in various dispensations received priesthood keys of sealing from Jesus Christ:

- "And I will give unto thee the keys of the kingdom of heaven: and whatsoever thou shalt bind on earth shall be bound in heaven . . ." (Matthew 16:19).
- "Behold, I give unto you power, that whatsoever ye shall seal on earth shall be sealed in heaven . . ." (Helaman 10:7).
- "I say unto you, that whatsoever you seal on earth shall be

> sealed in heaven; and whatsoever you bind on earth, in my name and by my word, saith the Lord, it shall be eternally bound in the heavens . . ." (D&C 132:46).

Every Saturday when I work in the temple, I witness individuals sealed to each other by sacred priesthood keys. An eighty-year-old man and his eighty-eight-year-old sister were sealed to their deceased parents. A couple came with their four adopted children to have the youngest sealed to them. A woman came to be sealed to her deceased husband, and then five adult children were sealed to them. The temple is the birthplace of eternal families. Men, women, and children can all reach out to the priesthood and be bound together for eternity. The priesthood is God's power to seal.

Multitudes of latter-day examples concerning the power of the priesthood in everyday life could be cited. After describing an occasion when Heber C. Kimball gave a blessing to his family, Elder Holland reminded us of what it means to have the priesthood in our lives: "That scene has been reenacted one way or another a thousand times, a hundred thousand times, in The Church of Jesus Christ of Latter-day Saints—a fear, a need, a call, a danger, a sickness, an accident, a death. I have been a participant in such moments. I have beheld the power of God manifest in my home and in my ministry. I have seen evil rebuked and the elements controlled. I know what it means to have mountains of difficulty move and ominous Red Seas part. I know what it means to have the destroying angel 'pass by them.' To have received the authority and to have exercised the power of 'the Holy Priesthood, after the Order of the Son of God,' is as great a blessing for me and for my family as I could ever hope for in this world. And that, in the end, is the meaning of the priesthood in everyday terms—its unequaled, unending, constant capacity to bless" (Holland, 43).

# FOR PARENTS WHO HAVE "LOST" CHILDREN

My sister Jeanette once found a quail hatchling that looked like it wouldn't survive. She took the minutes-old infant into the house and stood vigil as the hatchling clung to life. The tiny creature seemed to realize that its frail existence depended on this loving caregiver and trustingly laid its head on her thumb and slept in her hand or on her chest throughout the night. Occasionally, it opened its mouth a little, and Jeanette gave it a tiny drop of water or a bit of a crumb.

At about seven the next morning, the infant quail revived and began squawking and running around her bedroom, so she took the baby outside and put it under the bush where it had been born. The little quail uttered a sound as if it were calling someone. From about fifty feet away, a quail answered! The chick turned toward the sound, and the father quail flew down to meet it. Father and baby were reunited.

Some have had similar experiences nursing little ones through long and lonely nights. In some of those cases, there was no miracle in the morning, and a precious child was "lost" for a season. The intense grief a parent feels at such a loss can blur our vision so much that we don't see our baby call, Heavenly Father answer, and baby and Father reunite after only a brief separation.

The beautiful doctrine of the gospel of Jesus Christ concerning children who die before the age of accountability comforts the first grief of separation, changes it to acceptance ("Thy will be done") and eventually results in joy as parents age and anticipate their reunion with both Father and "lost" child. Bitterness becomes progressively sweet the closer the reunion gets. "Losing" a child to disease or accident, as traumatic and life-changing as it is, can unify parents in the cause of righteous living so they can merit the privilege of raising that child in the Millennium. There will yet be the miracle in the morning—not tomorrow morning, but in the morning of the First Resurrection.

Joseph and Emma Smith knew: "Death was no stranger in the Smith family, nor was it to any family in that era. Three of Joseph and Emma's children died in Kirtland, their own infant twins and their adopted son Joseph Murdock Smith. . . . In the summer of 1832, Joseph wrote to Emma: 'I was grieved to hear that Hiram had lost his little child. I think we can in some degree simpathise [sic] with him but we all must be reconsiled [sic] to our lots and Say the will of the Son be done.' It wasn't until January 1836 that Joseph's vision brought a new comfort to mothers and fathers who lost infant children: 'And I also beheld that all children who die before they arrive at the years of accountability, are saved in the celestial kingdom of heaven'" (Linda King Newell and Valeen Tippetts Avery, "Sweet Counsel and Seas of Tribulation: The Religious Life of the Women in Kirtland," *BYU Studies*, Vol. 20, No. 2: Winter 1980, 153-54).

Whenever a parent "loses" a child to death, pain of parting rips a hole in the heart. It's contrary to the natural order of life; parents should precede their children in death. But regardless of the age a child leaves this fragile existence, comfort can be found in the passing of a righteous child. Doctrinally speaking, both the child younger than age eight and the righteous child eight or older are saved, not "lost." After a brief season comes reunion.

There is a different kind of "loss" where comforting words cannot be so easily found. A dear friend recently received the devastating news that her son had done something very wrong. When she told me, I cried with her as she sobbed, "He's lost. He's lost to us." She described how life seems surreal, how daytime tears become nighttime weeping. Each morning she puts a fresh towel under her husband's and her pillows and removes the damp ones.

I searched the scriptures, looking for hope to console her. In the New Testament, the Savior asks a question: "How think ye? if a man have an hundred sheep, and one of them be gone astray, doth he not leave the ninety and nine, and goeth into the mountains, and seeketh that which is gone astray?" (Matthew 18:12). "Gone astray" is different than "lost." "Lost" seems irreversible. "Gone astray" leaves room for hope.

Hope that, like the quail, your loved one will one day receive the drop of saving water, the crumb of repentance, and "that which went astray" will call on the name of his Father and that the Father will answer. Then the heavens and earth will rejoice. For if "he find it, verily I say unto you, he rejoiceth more of that sheep, than of the ninety and nine which went not astray" (Matthew 18:13).

Most importantly, we learn from the scriptures that a parent does not search alone for the child who has "gone astray." The Good Shepherd—who loves the sheep more than any of us can, who has more capacity to love than any of us has, and who has much more experience in search and rescue—has left the "ninety and nine" secure in the fold and is looking in the "mountains" for "that which is gone astray."

"For the Son of man is come to save that which was lost" (Matthew 18:11), we are assured. And despite the loss that currently hurts so profoundly, "Weeping may endure for a night, but joy cometh in the morning" (Psalms 30:5).

# WHERE CAN I FIND HEALING?

Like most of you, I have a number of credit cards in my wallet. A silver one gives me one percent back on all purchases; a blue one gives me five percent back on groceries; a black one gives five percent back on gas and auto repairs. Each card has my name on it and the name of the company who is extending its credit to me. Each card has a credit limit, so I can't charge over a certain amount. But my most important credit card isn't a colored plastic card in my wallet. It is a divine credit card that bears both my name and the name of Him whose credit I am allowed to use.

As I understand the Atonement of Jesus Christ, every person who has ever lived or will ever live upon the earth is issued such a credit card. His omniscience grants an unbelievable credit limit; however, I can impose my own limit on my available credit. The Savior explained this doctrine in a parable.

There was a servant who owed ten thousand talents, which is equal to millions of dollars today. He couldn't pay the debt, so the master commanded that he, his wife, and his children be sold into slavery. The servant fell down and begged for forgiveness of the debt. At that point the master was moved with compassion, forgave the debt, and let the man go.

This same servant then went out and found a fellow servant who owed him a hundred pence, which is equal to mere pennies today. He grabbed his fellow servant by the throat and demanded payment. The fellow servant could not pay the debt and begged for mercy. But the servant who had just been forgiven millions refused to forgive pennies, and he had the fellow servant thrown into prison until he could pay the debt.

When the master heard about the servant's behavior, he "said unto him, O thou wicked servant, I forgave thee all that debt, because thou desiredst me:

"Shouldest not thou also have had compassion on thy fellow servant, even as I had pity on thee?

"And his lord was wroth, and delivered him to the tormentors, till he should pay all that was due unto him.

"So likewise shall my heavenly Father do also unto you, if ye from your hearts forgive not every one his brother their trespasses" (Matthew 18:32–35). What does this mean for us? If we don't forgive others as the Savior has forgiven us, we have to pay the debt for our sins ourselves.

A few years ago, a woman I'll call Elizabeth received a letter asking her to speak at BYU Women's Conference. Elizabeth was flattered and prepared prayerfully, but she was confused. The assigned topic seemed unusual and was difficult for her to define.

Elizabeth wondered why she had been asked to speak on that particular topic but finally decided it was because she grew up with an alcoholic father. She decided her purpose was to teach the sisters how to deal with adversity by being strong. She spent the next three months perfecting her talk and eventually had memorized it almost word-for-word. In the talk she told about the resentment she felt toward her father, how she had learned to bravely cope, and how much trauma she still had to bear because of him. The night before her presentation she went to sleep feeling well prepared. In the middle of the night, however, she awoke as a voice said four words to her: "You don't know everything."

The next day at Women's Conference she stood before an auditorium packed to overflowing and explained that for months she had been preparing the wrong talk. She told how she had planned to talk about the irreparable harm her father had caused her and her family. But instead, she would be speaking without notes, from her heart, because of what she had experienced the previous the night. Then she tearfully spoke of the message in the night and her realization that she had been judgmental and unforgiving. She now knew that she didn't understand her father because, as the voice said, she "didn't know everything."

As she had been on her way to Provo that morning, frantic that she didn't have a talk, she had humbly prayed, "Since I can't give my prepared talk, what shall I say?" The Spirit whispered, "Tell the good things about your father." She had forgotten that there *were* good things. As she spoke with a softened heart, she remembered his good qualities and the good times they had shared. She realized how narrowly and inaccurately she had viewed him. The resentment that had built up over fifty years began melting. In her ward Relief Society the following Sunday, she told of the change of heart she had experienced because she had finally forgiven him.

Elizabeth and you and I are all fellow servants who go around trying to extract apologies and reparations from those who trespass against us; when we do that, our credit card limit suffers. When we forgive as we have been forgiven, our credit card again has no maximum limit. Elizabeth now realizes that not only does she not know everything about her father, she doesn't know everything about anyone else. The voice taught her to forgive and let go, to move past the bad and focus on the good. The Savior had already paid for her father's sins and for her pains—she just had to realize it.

On the next to last page of *The Hiding Place,* Christian holocaust survivor Corrie Ten Boom tells about meeting one of the most malicious guards from Ravensbrück, the only major Nazi concentration camp for women. An estimated 92,000 died there, including Corrie's sister Betsie. After the war Corrie went on tour, speaking about forgiveness in various church services. She wrote:

"It was at a church service in Munich that I saw him, the former S.S. man who had stood guard at the shower room door in the processing center at Ravensbruck. He was the first of our actual jailers that I had seen since that time. And suddenly it was all there—the roomful of mocking men, the heaps of clothing, Betsie's pain-blanched face.

"He came up to me as the church was emptying, beaming and bowing, 'How grateful I am for your message, Fraulein' he said. 'To think that, as you say, He has washed my sins away!'

"His hand was thrust out to shake mine. And I, who had preached so often to the people . . . The need to forgive, kept my hand at my side.

"Even as the angry, vengeful thoughts boiled through me, I saw the sin of them. Jesus Christ had died for this man; was I going to ask for more? Lord Jesus, I prayed, forgive me and help me to forgive him.

"I tried to smile, I struggled to raise my hand. I could not. I felt nothing, not the slightest spark of warmth or charity. And so again I breathed a silent prayer. Jesus, I cannot forgive him. Give me Your forgiveness.

"As I took his hand the most incredible thing happened. From my shoulder along my arm and through my hand a current seemed to pass from me to him, while into my heart sprang a love for this stranger that almost overwhelmed me.

"And so I discovered that it is not on our forgiveness any more than on our goodness that the world's healing hinges, but on His. When He tells us to love our enemies, He gives, along with the command, the love itself" (Corrie Ten Boom, *The Hiding Place* [New York: Bantam Books, 1971], 238).

With the chastising phrase, "you don't know everything," Elizabeth was helped to accept correction and let the resentment go in order to fully activate the Atonement in her life. Corrie experienced the same cleansing when the current of love sprang from her heart and allowed her to shake the hand of her Ravensbrück abuser. Elizabeth and Corrie discovered for themselves the miracle of forgiveness, which is healing.

Where can we find healing? Luke, the physician, tells us, "A great multitude . . . came to hear him, and to be healed of their diseases. . . .

". . . they that were vexed with unclean spirits . . . were healed.

"And the whole multitude sought to touch him . . . and [he] healed them all" (Luke 6:17–19). Only in and through the limitless and boundless love of Jesus Christ can we be healed. "The Son of God suffereth according to the flesh that he might take upon him the sins of his people, that he might blot out their transgressions according to the power of his deliverance; and now behold [said Alma], this is the testimony which is in me" (Alma 7:13). May it also be the testimony in all of us.

# THE ANGEL TOOK BACK THE PLATES

"Yeah, right," is the look I often see on the faces of visitors to the Museum of Church History and Art when I explain that Moroni took back the plates after they were translated. "Sure," their faces seem to say. "Nice try."

As a docent, my museum name badge gives me access to many visitors who have never heard that Joseph Smith received from Moroni the plates that he translated, and that the record became the Book of Mormon. As I'm telling the story, most show interest until I come to the part where Moroni takes the plates back.

At first I didn't know how to respond, but the Spirit has helped me verbalize visitors' thoughts. "I know you are thinking, 'An angel delivered a book written on gold plates, and an angel took back a book written on gold plates. How convenient.'" The visitor nods, smiles shyly, and listens again. And then I say something such as, "It would be in the fairytale range if it weren't for the fact that there were others besides Joseph Smith who saw and touched the gold plates. Some even saw the angel. This fulfills the law of witnesses as prescribed in the scriptures: 'In the mouth of two or three witnesses every word may be established' (Matthew 18:16). The law of witnesses ratifies Heavenly Father's work."

We know that there are many witnesses.

**Witness #1: The Holy Ghost.** How many witnesses does it take to confirm the story of an ancient record engraved on gold plates, buried in a hill, delivered by an angel, and translated by an uneducated farm boy? The answer is, only one—the Holy Ghost. But there are many more.

**Witness #2: The Book of Mormon.** The fact that the Book of Mormon exists is in itself a witness. The fact that it contains a test whereby every reader can know it is the word of God is compelling.

**Witness #3: The Prophet Joseph Smith.** Joseph Smith received the plates of gold from Moroni, an angelic messenger sent from the presence of God. He translated this ancient record by the gift and power of God and spent the rest of his life testifying of the Book of Mormon. Said he: "I told the Brethren that the Book of Mormon is the most correct of any book on earth, and the keystone of our religion, and a man would get nearer to God by abiding its precepts, than by any other book" (*History of the Church,* 4:461).

**Witnesses #4, #5, and #6: David Whitmer, Oliver Cowdery, and Martin Harris.** These three men give their testimonies to the world, as printed in the Book of Mormon. They affirm that Moroni, an angelic personage sent from the presence of God, showed them the gold plates. Despite the fact that all three men left the Church (two later returned), they never denied their testimonies. Since David Whitmer is the one of the Three Witnesses who did not return to the Church, the following transcript of an interview with him is especially important:

> I saw them [the plates and other artifacts] just as plain as I see this bed (striking his hand upon the bed beside him). I heard the voice of the Angel just as stated in said Book, and the engravings on the plates were shown to us, and we were commanded to bear record of them; and if they are not true, then there is no truth. . . . I have been asked if we saw those things with our natural eyes. Of course they were our natural eyes. There is no doubt that our eyes were prepared for the sight, but they were our natural eyes nevertheless.
>
> Rather suggestively [Colonel Giles] asked if it might not have been possible that he, Mr. Whitmer, had been mistaken and had simply been moved upon by some mental disturbance, or hallucination, which had deceived them into *thinking* he saw the

> Personage, the Angel, the plates, the Urim and Thummim, and the sword of Laban.
>
> How well and distinctly I remember the manner in which Elder Whitmer arose and drew himself up to his full height—a little over six feet—and said, in solemn and impressive tones:
>
> "No sir! I was not under any hallucination, nor was I deceived! I saw with these eyes, and I heard with these ears! I know whereof I speak!" (Richard Lloyd Anderson, *Investigating the Book of Mormon Witnesses* [Salt Lake City: Deseret Book Company, 1981], 88)

David Whitmer died January 25, 1888. The next day, the *Richmond Democrat* printed this obituary: "On the evening of Sunday, January 22, at half past five o'clock, Mr. Whitmer called his family and a number of his friends to his bedside, and to them delivered his dying testimony. . . .

"Now you must all be faithful in Christ. I want to say to you all that the Bible and the Record of the Nephites (the Book of Mormon), are true, so you can say that you have heard me bear my testimony on my death bed'" (B. H. Roberts, *New Witnesses for God,* Vol. 2 [Salt Lake City: Deseret News, 1909], 262).

**Witnesses #7 through #14: Christian Whitmer, Jacob Whitmer, Peter Whitmer, Jun., John Whitmer, Hiram Page, Joseph Smith, Sr., Samuel H. Smith, and Hyrum Smith.** The testimony of these eight men is also printed in the Book of Mormon. They state that they did "handle" and "heft" the plates. Like the Three Witnesses, these Eight Witnesses reaffirmed what they had seen throughout their lives. For example, published in the *Deseret News* was a conversation between John Whitmer and P. Wilhelm Poulson:

> I [P. Wilhelm Poulson]: I am aware that your name is affixed to the testimony in the Book of Mormon, that you saw the plates?
>
> He [John Whitmer]: It is so, and that testimony is true.
>
> I: Did you handle the plates with your hands?

> He: I did so!
> I: Then they were a material substance?
> He: Yes, as material as anything can be.
> I: Were they heavy to lift?
> He: Yes, and as you know gold is a heavy metal: they were very heavy.
> I: How big were the leaves?
> He: So far as I recollect, 8 by 6 or 7 inches.
> I: Were the leaves thick?
> He: Yes, just so thick, that characters could be engraven on both sides.
> I: How were the leaves joined together?
> He: In three rings, each one in the shape of a D with the straight line towards the center.
> I: In what place did you see the plates?
> He: In Joseph Smith's house; he had them there.
> I: Did you see them covered with a cloth?
> He: No. He handed them uncovered into our hands, and we turned the leaves sufficient to satisfy us. (*Deseret News,* August 6, 1878)

**Witness #15: Lucy Smith.** "From [the time Moroni began tutoring Joseph about Nephite and Lamanite cultures and the doctrines so clearly taught in the Book of Mormon] . . . every evening we gathered our children together and gave our time up to the discussion of those things which he instructed to us. I think that we presented the most peculiar aspect of any family that ever lived upon the earth, all seated in a circle, father, mother, sons, and daughters, listening in breathless anxiety to the religious teachings of a boy eighteen years of age who had never read the Bible through by course in his life" (Scot Facer Proctor and Maurine Jensen Proctor, eds., *The History of Joseph Smith Revised and Enhanced* [Salt Lake City: Bookcraft, Inc., 1996], 111).

**Witness #16: William Smith.** "I was permitted to lift [the plates] as they laid in a pillow case; but not to see them, as it was contrary to the commands [Joseph] had received. They weighed about sixty pounds according to my best judgment. . . . They were not quite as large as this Bible. . . . One could easily tell that they were not stone, hewn out to deceive, or even a block of wood. . . . [T]hey were much heavier than stone and very much heavier than wood" (Milton V. Bachman Jr., *Eyewitness Accounts of the Restoration* [Salt Lake City: Deseret Book Company, 1986], 70).

**Witness #17: Emma Smith.** "[During the translation] the plates often lay on the [table in our home] without any attempt at concealment, wrapped in a small linen table cloth, which I had given him to fold them in. I once felt of the plates, as they thus lay on the table, tracing their outline and shape. They seemed to be pliable like thick paper, and would rustle with a metallic sound when the edges were moved by the thumb, as one does sometimes thumb the edges of the book. . . .

"I did not attempt to handle the plates, other than [through the linen cloth]" (*Testimonies of Book of Mormon Witnesses,* 290, and "Last Testimony of Sister Emma," *The Saints' Herald* 26 [October 1879], 289–90).

**Witness #18: Katherine Smith Salisbury.** "[Katherine said that] Joseph allowed her to 'heft' the package but not to see the gold plates, as the angel had forbidden him to show them at that period. She said they were very heavy" (Anderson, *Investigating the Book of Mormon Witnesses,* 27).

**Witness #19: Mary Musselman Whitmer.** David Whitmer related that some time after this his mother (Mary Musselman Whitmer) "was going to milk the cows, when she was met out near the yard by the same old man (judging by her description of him) who said to her: 'You have been very faithful and diligent in your labors, but you are tried because of the increase of your toil; it is proper therefore that your faith may be strengthened.' Thereupon he showed her the plates. My father and mother had a large family of their own, the addition to it therefore of Joseph, his wife Emma and Oliver very greatly increased the toil and anxiety of my mother. And although she had never complained she had sometimes felt that her labor was too much, or at least she was beginning to feel so. This circumstance, however, completely removed all such feelings and nerved her up for her increased responsibilities" (*Contributor,* Vol. 5 [October 1883–September 1884], 404).

**Witness #20: YOU.** Moroni promises, "When [you] read these things . . . I would exhort you that [you] ask God, the Eternal Father, in the name of Christ, if these things are not true; and if [you] ask with a sincere heart, with real intent, having faith in Christ, he will manifest the truth of it unto you, by the power of the Holy Ghost" (Moroni 10:3–4).

With this knowledge, you can fulfill a Biblical prophecy. Speaking to Ezekiel, the Lord said, "Take thee one stick, and write upon it, For Judah, and for the children of Israel his companions [the Bible]: then take another stick, and write upon it, For Joseph, the stick of Ephraim, and *for* all the house of Israel his companions [the Book of Mormon]:

"And join them one to another into one stick; and they [these two books] shall become one in thine hand" (Ezekiel 37:16–17). Every week when you carry your Bible and Book of Mormon to church, you fulfill this prophecy.

The testimonies of these nineteen witnesses and your testimony combine with the testimonies of millions of Church members all over the world, collectively attesting that the Book of Mormon stands with the Bible as another testament that Jesus Christ is the Savior and Redeemer of all. All of us who have received the promised witness can do as Joseph Smith did and spend the rest of our lives testifying of the Book of Mormon, "the most correct of any book on earth" (Introduction to the Book of Mormon).

# LET ME SELL YOU SOME REAL ESTATE PART 1

A few years ago, Richard and I went on vacation with our son-in-law Terry, our daughter Michelle, and their four children. Through a point reward program, we had earned a week at what we anticipated was a magnificent resort in the middle of the Pacific Ocean. Since there were additional sites we wanted to see, we added a couple of days to the front of our itinerary at two different locations. It was my job to get these two hotel reservations. I wanted to get a place on a beach, if possible, that wasn't too pricey. I called a number of places and found a hotel, The Edgewater, which seemed amazingly reasonable. This is what I wrote in my journal:

"We arrived at The Edgewater, which is not on the edge of any water. The room, including the bathroom, was about twelve feet square. *Relic* would be a good descriptor. The elevator showed evidence that the doors had been pried open, wallpaper hung loose on the walls, the carpets were frayed, and the balcony was locked and looked as if it would collapse under a stray cat's weight. It was clean enough if you didn't take off your shoes or put your toothbrush down anywhere."

During that night, besides worrying about what was going to crawl on me, I thought about the Relief Society lesson I had to give when I returned home. The subject was the three degrees of glory, and it occurred to me that we were experiencing the hotel version of the telestial kingdom. Remembering the persuasive, smooth-talking salesperson who had convinced me to stay at The Edgewater, I decided to present the lesson as though I were a real estate salesman selling homes in the hereafter.

As members of the Church, we do not believe that good people go to heaven and bad people go to hell. We believe that everyone but a very few will inherit a kingdom of glory. As your friendly Realtor, I will preview the different kingdoms, neighborhoods, schools, and price tags for each community in which you can live hereafter. (Before we get started, I'll let you in on a trick of the real estate trade: We show clients the least desirable property first.) So here goes.

The first potential home site is in the telestial kingdom. The word *telestial* does not appear in the Bible, but only in latter-day revelation. *Telos* is a Greek word meaning "end." According to Richard O. Cowan, "Paul explained that there will be an orderly sequence in resurrections, beginning with that of Christ and continuing until the *telos,* or 'end' (see 1 Corinthians 15:21–24). Those individuals who have earned the right to live in the telestial kingdom will be the last going to a kingdom of glory to be resurrected." Brother Cowan feels "the name *telestial* may also be related to the prefix *tele-,* meaning 'far off' or 'distant.' The telestial kingdom will be the kingdom of glory most removed from the presence and glory of God" (Richard O. Cowan, *Answers to Your Questions About the Doctrine and Covenants* [Salt Lake City: Deseret Book Company, 1996], 91).

But don't let that dissuade you. The telestial kingdom is nicer than the most elegant vacation home on the most exotic isle here on earth. The Lord states in D&C 76:89 that the glory of the telestial kingdom "surpasses all understanding." It is definitely a kingdom of glory. Is it sounding like something you'd be interested in?

Before you make any decisions, let me tell you about your neighbors. They will be telestial beings just like you, either former members of the Church of Jesus Christ who broke covenants and willfully rejected the gospel while on earth, or the "liars, and sorcerers, and adulterers, and whoremongers" (D&C 76:103) who "receive[d] not the gospel, neither the testimony of Jesus, neither the prophets" (D&C 76:101) while on earth or after mortality.

One good thing about the telestial kingdom is that you will be able to have the influence of the Holy Ghost, but—and I have to be honest here—"where God and Christ dwell [you] cannot come" (D&C 76:112). Another good thing is that the telestial kingdom is compared to the brightness of the stars as viewed from earth, and the stars are very pretty on a clear night, don't you agree? I just love the way some of them twinkle, and there are so many of them.

The price tag for the telestial kingdom is very reasonable. While on earth, you don't have to contribute to a church and you can spend your Sundays doing whatever you like. You don't even have to *belong* to a church. You can enjoy eating and drinking and putting into or on your body whatever you choose. And you don't have to struggle with becoming disciplined or curtailing your appetites. Anything goes! And repentance? If you never really got into it, no worry. It's not required here for a long time because you won't come forth from the grave until the last resurrection, which leaves lots of time for repentance.

Now for the best part: I can guarantee you a place in the telestial kingdom. There's room for all—well, except the sons of perdition, and you don't have to worry about them. They'll be busy wailing and gnashing their teeth in some place called outer darkness, which I understand is a place without glory. But again, the telestial kingdom *is* a place of glory. You will have a resurrected body and live much better there than here on earth. By law, however, I must make you aware of some fine print in the contract. You may have to spend time in, well, a temporary location called spirit prison, but it's probably not as bad as it sounds.

On a lighter note, I bet you want to know what kind of employment is available in a telestial world. Besides working to overcome problems you had on earth and learning to live with your neighbors—who you'll recall were "liars, sorcerers, whoremongers, and adulterers" on earth—the people here get to be "servants of the Most High" (D&C 76:112). Wow! Everyone gets to be a servant! Oh, and there is one more thing. If you decide by the choices you make during your life to live in the telestial kingdom, I hope you don't want to be married or have children, because neither of those can happen in the telestial kingdom.

So, any takers?

# LET ME SELL YOU SOME REAL ESTATE PART 2

We stayed in The Edgewater just one night and happily made our way across the island to a place called the Best Inn, which is vintage 1950s. I thought it should be called the Better Inn because it definitely wasn't the *best,* but it was better than The Edgewater. As advertised, the Best Inn had a private beach. What the ad *didn't* mention was that you had to cross the main highway and walk about two blocks to get there. It was cleaner and bigger than The Edgewater. There were a few cockroach sightings and the hot water wouldn't turn on in the bathroom sink, but a continental breakfast was part of the deal. So all in all, it was a step up. That night I thought, "This is like the terrestrial kingdom!" Back to my lesson.

The next stop on our tour of potential home sites in the next life is the terrestrial kingdom. Now this is *better* real estate in many ways. First, terrestrial beings with terrestrial intelligence and terrestrial bodies will live here. No one telestial will be here. So if you're terrestrial, you'll fit right in. While translating John 5:29, Joseph Smith and Sidney Rigdon saw the terrestrial kingdom. Joseph Smith's account of this vision describes terrestrial persons as the honorable people of the earth who were not valiant in their testimonies of Jesus because they were blinded by the craftiness of men (see D&C 76:74–75, 77, 79).

These people will make quite nice neighbors, I'd think. And when all's said and done, I am confident you'll like living among such decent, friendly people. President Spencer W. Kimball described them as "lukewarm," which I figure means they are pretty low-key. President Kimball said, "Lukewarm Saints get terrestrial glory. . . . The 'unvaliant' Latter-day Saint will find himself there" (Edward L.

Kimball, ed., *Teachings of Spencer W. Kimball* [Salt Lake City: Bookcraft, Inc., 1982], 48), which I interpret to mean that you don't have to live the commandments fully while on earth. If you want to be terrestrial, you don't have to pay tithing if it's inconvenient or if you need the money for something else. As for fast offerings, well, you'll only want to give if you need a tax write-off. You'll want to attend church sometimes, but if there's a championship sports game on television on Sunday, by all means, stay home to watch it. Or when you are on vacation, make it a real vacation by vacationing from your meetings, too. There will always be another sacrament meeting next week.

The price tag for this upscale neighborhood is moderate as far as commitment to callings. Yes, you may be expected to accept callings in your ward and stake, but you don't have to accept any calling that will be inconvenient or that doesn't fit your personality or image. And that part about magnifying callings—no worry. How and when and if you serve is up to you. *Sacrifice* and *consecration* are not words that apply in this kingdom.

The terrestrial is definitely more prestigious than the telestial, for those who live here will "receive the presence of the Son" (D&C 76:77), which seems to mean you will be visited from time to time by Jesus Christ. You'll recall that in the telestial world you'll have the influence of the Holy Ghost, but here you'll have the influence of the Son of God! But again, I believe in full disclosure, so I must tell you that in the terrestrial world you will not receive "the fulness of the Father" (verse 77).

The glory of the terrestrial is likened to that of the moon as seen from earth, and personally, I really like a nice full moon on a crisp October evening—well, even crescent moons are lovely. "Wherefore, they are bodies terrestrial, and not bodies celestial, and differ in glory as the moon differs from the sun" (D&C 76:78).

Another very good aspect of the terrestrial kingdom that I must mention is that you have guaranteed employment. Get this: You will be "angels of God forever and ever" (D&C 132:17), and I understand the benefits are great! Joseph Smith and Sidney Rigdon said, "And thus we saw the glory of the terrestrial which excels in all things the glory of the telestial, even in glory, and in power, and in might, and in dominion" (D&C 76:91).

The same fine print that I briefly mentioned in my description of the telestial world applies to the terrestrial world as well. Membership in the terrestrial club is for adults only who are not interested in procreation. Terrestrial people "remain separately and singly . . . to all eternity" (D&C 132:17). No marriage. No children.

What do you think? Ready to sign on?

# LET ME SELL YOU SOME REAL ESTATE PART 3

When we left the Best Inn we flew to our last destination, the resort that was supposed to be awesome. But by now, I was panicked. What if the resort was another Edgewater? A person I met while staying at the Best Inn said someone she knew stayed at the resort we were going to and it was really run down. I adjusted my expectations down a few notches, but I hoped the resort would be at least slightly better than the Best Inn.

As we turned onto the resort property, I took a deep breath as we entered a tropical paradise and drove for a mile before we saw the hotel itself and the private beach at the same time. There were fountains, flowers, waterfalls, a five-leaf-clover-shaped swimming pool, bridges, and walkways shaded by flowering plants where swans, geese, and ducks roamed. Foot-long golden fish swam in perfectly manicured ponds. The lobby featured marble floors, palms, and gigantic fresh floral arrangements. The uniformed resort staff treated us as though they had been anxiously awaiting our arrival.

After we checked in, we were taken to our suite. Dazzled by the view as we opened the door, Terry voiced our joint enthusiasm: "Now *this* is how I want to live!" Things here came in threes—three balconies, three refrigerators, three giant televisions. Elegance in every detail surprised and delighted us.

By the time Monday night arrived, I volunteered to give the family home evening lesson because I'd formulated my thoughts enough to give a lesson on the three degrees of glory (as practice for my Relief Society lesson). After comparing and contrasting the three places we had stayed in, I summarized by asking the children where they wanted to live for eternity and with whom they wanted to live. They quickly said they wanted to live at the resort with everyone they knew and loved. I concluded by suggesting that in the future, whenever a temptation came, if they considered that the consequence might be staying eternally in The Edgewater, they'd not succumb to the temptation. I asked them if they would consider the Best Inn. No, they didn't want to live there either. They wanted the resort.

I did remind them that the celestial kingdom was not going to be like one continual vacation. Yes, it would be an absolutely indescribably beautiful place to live, but it would not be a place where inhabitants will just lounge around. In fact, people in every kingdom will have work to do. Everyone will work and work hard to help Heavenly Father and Jesus Christ "bring to pass the immortality and eternal life of man" (Moses 1:39). Their work and glory will become our work and glory. What a privilege!

Back to being your real estate broker of the future:

The third stop on our future home tour ends with the celestial kingdom. This is an exclusive, gated community with rigorous entry requirements and an expensive price tag. Tithing and fast offerings are not all that's required. You'll have to give not only of your time and means, but also of your broken heart and your contrite spirit. You must also be willing to keep your baptismal and temple covenants.

In the celestial kingdom you'll find people who have a testimony of Jesus and who worked to build the kingdom of God while on earth. They had faith in Jesus Christ, repented of their sins, were baptized by immersion, received the Holy Ghost by the laying on of hands, and endured to the end in righteousness. You'll recall how the influence of the Holy Ghost governs the telestial and the influence of the Savior governs the terrestrial? Well, here in the celestial, all who attain this kingdom "shall dwell in the presence of God and his Christ forever and ever" (D&C 76:62).

An interesting feature of the celestial kingdom is that it contains three levels or kingdoms: "In the celestial glory there are three heavens or degrees;

"And in order to obtain the highest, a man must enter into this order of the priesthood [meaning the new and everlasting covenant of marriage];

"And if he does not, he cannot obtain it.

"He may enter into the other, but that is the end of his kingdom; he cannot have an increase" (D&C 131:1–4).

What *increase* means, according to Joseph Smith, is that couples married for eternity who complete all other requirements to enter the highest level of the celestial kingdom will be able to bear spirit children after mortal life. "Except a man and his wife enter into an everlasting covenant and be married for eternity . . . by the power and authority of the Holy Priesthood, they will cease to increase when they die; that is, they will not have any children after the resurrection" (Joseph Fielding Smith, *Teachings of the Prophet Joseph Smith* [Salt Lake City: Deseret Book Company, 1976], 300–301). Simply put, in the highest degree of the celestial kingdom you can have an intimate relationship with your spouse and have the joy of conceiving and bearing children throughout all eternity. The ability to procreate is the privilege of the gods. Those who achieve the highest level in the celestial kingdom are on their way to becoming gods, which means they are exalted and become "joint-heirs with Jesus Christ" (Romans 8:17), receiving all that the Father has.

Other residents of the celestial kingdom will include Adam and Eve and their righteous children; Enoch and his people who were translated; Noah and his wife; Abraham and Sarah and their faithful posterity; Moses, Isaiah, Daniel, Ezekiel, and their righteous wives and children; Lehi and Sariah and their children who loved the Lord; Alma the Elder and Younger; Helaman, Ether, Mormon, and Moroni; John the Baptist; Peter, James, and John and all the other Apostles and disciples on both continents who served Jesus Christ when He was on the earth, and their posterity who loved God and served their fellow men. Also in residence will be Joseph Smith, Brigham Young, the other latter-day prophets and Apostles, and all men and women who kept their covenants throughout all generations. Not only that, but you will live by many of your ancestors for whom you did research and temple work. And there's more good news! *All* children who died before the age of accountability (eight) live here as well—and it is to be hoped that your parents, spouse, children, and grandchildren will live here in unspeakable joy with you!

There are two last aspects about life in the celestial kingdom of which I should make you aware. First, you may have noticed that I didn't mention anything about the schools in the other two kingdoms. That's because I don't know about the telestial or terrestrial school systems, but I do know about the celestial school district. Everyone—yes, everyone—who inherits the celestial kingdom receives a white stone. "Then the white stone mentioned in Revelation 2:17, will become a Urim and Thummim to each individual who receives one, whereby things pertaining to a higher order of kingdoms will be made known" (D&C 130:10). The white stone—probably a celestial version of the fastest, most comprehensive computer imaginable—will teach celestial beings all things. *All* is impressively inclusive.

Before you decide which property is right for you, I feel as your Realtor that I must share one more bit of information. Sometimes when I show the celestial kingdom to potential buyers, I notice some become discouraged about the price, and this happens in a way about which I'd like to forewarn you. I've been told that after hearing my presentation about the celestial world, a disparaging voice begins to dissuade potential property owners by saying, "You'll never make it; you're too flawed; don't even bother to try." I would like to caution you against listening to that voice. I know who is speaking. I know he wants you to be as miserable as he is. He knows nothing of joy. He has no wife and no children. No one ever calls him "Sweetheart" or "Daddy." His seductive voice is especially effective in dissuading and dispiriting women. Through discouragement, he convinces women that they have to be perfect to gain the celestial kingdom. He tries to block thoughts of the Atonement from entering your mind. Do not believe him. He is known for his cunning deceit. He has been a liar from the beginning.

Apostle Marvin J. Ashton cautioned us against giving up: "I believe that one of the great myths [you] would do well to dispel is that [you've] come to earth to perfect [yourself], and nothing short of that will do. . . .

"I am also convinced that the speed with which [you] head along the straight and narrow path isn't as important as the direction in which [you] are traveling . . . if it is leading toward eternal goals" (Marvin J. Ashton, *Measure of Our Hearts* [Salt Lake City: Deseret Book Company, 1991], 10).

President Wilford Woodruff said: "I have always said and believed, and I believe today, that it will pay you and me and all the sons and all the daughters of Adam to abide the celestial law, for celestial glory is worth all we possess; if it calls for every dollar we own and our lives into the bargain, if we obtain an entrance into the celestial kingdom of God it will amply repay us. The Latter-day Saints have started out for celestial glory, and if we can only manage to be faithful enough to obtain an inheritance in the kingdom, where God and Christ dwell, we shall rejoice through the endless ages of eternity" (*Journal of Discourses,* 17: 250–251).

This ends our parade of future home sites. This comparison of things earthly to things eternal is, of course, simplistic, because "eye hath not seen, nor ear heard, neither have entered into the heart of man, the things which God hath prepared for them that love him" (1 Corinthians 2:9). Oh, how I hope you and I, our families, and our friends will receive the same promise the Savior gave to the three Nephites: "ye shall sit down in the kingdom of my Father; [and] yea, your joy shall be full . . ." (3 Nephi 28:10).

# THE GOSPEL IS NOT A CAFETERIA LINE

Some members of the Church approach keeping the commandments as though these commandments were items in a cafeteria line. They say, "This looks good; I'll have this and this, but none of that, thanks." Dr. Hugh Nibley described such a person:

"A prosperous member of a ward . . . was wont to say that what he liked best about the gospel was that it was just like a cafeteria, where you could take what you want and leave what you want. Some maintain that by making a substantial contribution they are keeping the law of consecration. But if I keep only *some* of the Ten Commandments, I am not keeping the Ten Commandments; if I pay *some* of my tithing I am not paying tithing; if I keep the law of obedience, doing things God's way, when I find it convenient, I am not keeping that law; a person who is chaste some of the time is not keeping the law of chastity; if I part with odds and ends from time to time, I am not observing the law of sacrifice; a minifast of say twenty minutes or so between meals is not fasting" (Hugh Nibley, *Approaching Zion* [Salt Lake City: Deseret Book Company, and Provo, Utah: Foundation for Ancient Research and Mormon Studies, 1989], 392).

The gospel is not a pick-and-choose cafeteria but an endless smorgasbord where the more we partake, the more is given. The gospel of Jesus Christ is all about obedience. Joseph Smith said: "We cannot keep all the commandments without first knowing them, and we cannot expect to know all, or more than we now know unless we comply with or keep those we have already received" (*History of the Church,* 5:135).

In 1833, Joseph Smith organized the School of the Prophets to teach doctrines and principles of the gospel to leaders of the fledgling church. The school was held in an upstairs room in Newel K. Whitney's store. Joseph also had use of another room above the store, which was referred to as the translation room.

On the day the Prophet received what is now Section 89 of the Doctrine and Covenants, Zebedee Coltrin recalled: "When the Word of Wisdom was first presented by the Prophet Joseph (as he came out of the translating room) and was read to the School [of the Prophets], there were twenty out of the twenty-one [men in the room] who used tobacco and they all immediately threw their tobacco and pipes into the fire" (Minutes, Salt Lake School of Prophets, 13 Oct. 1883, 55–56). That's obedience!

There are other stirring examples of obedience in Church history. The Kirtland Saints were very poor when the revelation came to Joseph Smith to build a temple. As the leaders discussed the cost of building materials, they decided to build the temple out of logs. The Prophet Joseph responded: "Shall we, brethren, build a house for our God of logs? No, brethren, I have a better plan than that. I have the plan of the house of the Lord, given by Himself. You will see by this the difference between our calculations and His ideas." When the Lord's plan was made clear (see D&C 95:13–17), they responded with obedience and chose a site. Immediately Hyrum Smith ran to get a scythe to begin clearing the land for construction, exclaiming, "We are preparing to build a house for the Lord and I am determined to be the first at the work" (*The History of Lucy Mack Smith*, Church Archives). That's enthusiastic obedience.

Joseph Smith said, "The object with me is to obey and teach others to obey God in just what He tells us to do. It mattereth not whether the principle is popular or unpopular, I will always maintain a true principle, even if I stand alone in it" (*History of the Church,* 6:223).

You've heard the story of a Church member telling a nonmember how our prophet communicates God's will to His people. The nonmember thought that was wonderful and asked, "Well, what has your prophet said recently?" The member thought and thought but couldn't remember anything specific.

How can we obey counsel or instruction we don't recall? Obeying involves listening—to prophets, living and dead—because every commandment, every doctrine, and every principle is given for our good, both here and hereafter. How we listen to and obey the prophet is a personal measure of how much we love our eternal Father.

The power in obedience combines your love to obey with His love to bless, and the blessings *do* always follow. It's an eternal law. Attached to every commandment is a blessing. The Lord said, "There is a law, irrevocably decreed in heaven . . . upon which all blessings are predicated—

"And when [you] obtain any blessing from God, it is by obedience to that law upon which it is predicated" (D&C 130:20–21).

When we obey God, we give the only thing we can really give Him—everything else is already His. The cafeteria approach to the gospel limits our blessings. Let's not pick and choose the commandments we obey. Let's throw our pipes and tobacco into the fireplace and be the first with a tool at the temple site!

PHOTO BY JOHN W. LINFORD

# ABOUT THE AUTHOR

Marilynne Todd Linford has written eight other books: *ABCs for Young LDS, I Hope They Call Me on a Mission Too!, Is Anyone Out There Building Mother's Self-Esteem?, Slim for Life, Breast Cancer—Support Group in a Book, A Woman Fulfilled, Give Mom a Standing Ovation,* and *Sisters in Zion.* She and her husband, Richard, have eight children and nineteen grandchildren. She enjoys studying LDS Church history and serves as a docent in the Church Museum of History and Art. She serves in the Salt Lake Temple and on the Materials Evaluation Committee of the Church. Her hobbies include playing piano duets and Scrabble with anyone who is willing. For her, life's most beautiful moments include being with Richard and any combination of family at Church or national historic sites, on beaches where the air and water are the same warm temperature, or hiking the red rock canyons of Southern Utah.